Southern-Fried Philosophy
and Georgia Ice Cream

Charles E. Cravey

In His Steps Publishing

ISBN: 978-1-58535-062-9 (PAPER)

ISBN: 978-1-58535-063-6 (KINDLE)

ISBN: 978-1-58535-064-3 (HARD)

Library of Congress Catalog Number: 2025908371

Printed in the United States of America

Book Cover by Charles E. Cravey and Book Brush

Contents

Dedication   V

Preface   VII

Prologue   IX

1. The Art of Understanding   1

2. The Roads That Carry Us   39

3. The Philosophy of a Southern Life   85

4. Philosophy in Motion   127

5. The Bridge Forward   137

6. The Heart of Purpose   147

7. The Wisdom of Seasons   155

8. Grace and Gratitude   161

9. The Light Within   167

10. A Life Well Lived   173

Epilogue   181

About the author   184

To my dear mentor and friend,

Dr. Roger Branch.

May the philosophies discussed in this book

Make you proud of me after all these years!

I love you, Brother.

Preface

Nestled in the heart of middle Georgia, where time ambles along like the lazy drift of a fishing bobber in a quiet creek, lies the town where I was born. It was the place folks never wrote stories about—unless you counted the whispered gossip shared by church ladies after Sunday service. Not a soul of note ever passed through, save the Baptist and Methodist ministers who preached with fervor, or the county Sheriff whose name carried weight like the humid air in July.

Most people here reckoned they'd spend their whole lives in this one-horse town, where dreams took root but rarely grew tall. The cemeteries, scattered like forgotten pieces of a puzzle, held the stories of men and women who toiled under a Southern sun, their lives bound by hard work and grit.

Education, now—that was something you might stumble upon down at the service station, where the good ol' boys spun yarns about life and living. Or maybe sitting on the hood of a beat-up car parked at the edge of a backwoods cemetery, with the scent of pine and red Georgia clay in the air. It wasn't textbook learning, but it had a wisdom about it—Southern candor, seasoned with the salt and pepper of life.

This book is my tribute to those early days. They taught me lessons that no classroom ever could.

Now, I ought to warn you about the way I tell my tales. The language you'll find here is "country" and "Southern," pure as the sweet tea you'll find on any kitchen table south of the Mason-Dixon. I make no apologies for it, but some words might leave you scratching your head. Take the title, for instance—"Georgia Ice Cream." For those uninitiated in the ways of the South, it's just another name for cheese-grits, served warm and creamy, a comfort that sticks to your ribs and soothes your soul. If you've never had a bowl, well, you're missin' a bit of heaven.

So, pull up a chair and sit a spell—I hope you enjoy what's inside.

The Rev. Dr. Charles E. Cravey, April 2025

Prologue

A Journey Through the In-Between

Life starts with a cry—a first breath that sets us on a path so winding and unpredictable, it's a wonder we ever try to make sense of it. But that's just what we do, isn't it? Folks down here know all about life's rhythm: seasons changing, hands shaking, hearts breaking, and the sun setting, only to rise again. Between that first wail of a newborn and the last whisper of a life well-lived, there's a whole world of stories and lessons just waitin' to be told.

Now, don't get me wrong. I'm not here to hand out answers tied up in a neat little bow. No sir, life's far too messy for that. This book? Well, it's more like a porch swing conversation on a slow summer evening—an invitation to sit a spell, ponder awhile, and maybe see yourself in the stories I tell. It's about the big things—life, death, and what it means to truly live—but told the way we do in these parts: honest, heartfelt, and maybe with a little twang.

You see, down here, we've got a way of seeing the world that's equal parts practical and poetic. Life's as simple as a warm biscuit and as mysterious as the fireflies flickering in the pines. We reckon with death not by fearing it, but by making sure we've lived a life worth remembering. And as for living? Well, it's about finding joy in the small things, sharing a kind word with a neighbor, and carrying a little bit of hope in your pocket.

So, pull up a chair, y'all. Let's talk about what it means to live fully, to love deeply, and to leave behind something that matters. This is not a roadmap—it's a reflection, a meandering walk down memory lane, and a celebration of the precious moments that make up the in-between. Together, let's find the beauty in that fragile, fleeting space between the first breath and the last whisper.

1

The Art of Understanding

❧

"*You never really understand a person until you consider things from his point of view... Until you climb inside of his skin and walk around in it.*"
– Harper Lee, *To Kill a Mockingbird*

Growing up in the South, we learn quick that understanding folks isn't about knowing their names or where they come from—it's about walking a mile in their shoes, even if those shoes are worn thin with stories we'll never fully know. Life, at its best, is about connection. And connection begins with a simple truth: seeing the world through someone else's eyes.

This chapter is all about understanding—not just others, but ourselves. It's about learning the art of empathy, the wisdom of muted observation, and the beauty of setting aside judgment long enough to discover what lies in the heart of another. And when we do, we find that life, in all its complexity, becomes a little simpler—one shared smile, one kind word, one heartfelt conversation at a time.

Here in Georgia, there's a certain rhythm to life—a slow pace that gives you time to sit a spell and really listen, not just to what folks say, but to what they mean. It's that rhythm, that pause, that invites us to climb into someone else's skin for a while, just like Miss Harper Lee said.

We'll explore stories of understanding—moments when simple gestures transformed lives, when seeing the world through someone else's eyes brought clarity and compassion. And along the way, I'll share reflections on how empathy isn't just a gift we give others; it's a gift we give ourselves. Because to understand is to grow, and to grow is to live.

What is Philosophy? A Companion for Life

Philosophy is not about fancy words or dusty books left on tall shelves, though you might find some wisdom tucked away there if you're looking for it. It's something simpler, something rooted in the soil of everyday life. It's how we question, how we reflect, and how we strive to understand this peculiar thing called existence. Philosophy, at its heart, is a friend—a guide that walks beside us, helping us make sense of the world, no matter how tangled or untidy it gets.

In this chapter, we'll explore philosophy as more than theories spun out by thinkers long gone; instead, it's a living, breathing way of being. It's in the farmer who ponders the rhythm of the seasons, the mother who reflects on what it means to love deeply, and the neighbor who asks himself why kindness matters in a hurried world. To philosophize is to live intentionally—and intentionally living is how we find meaning.

Why Philosophy Matters

Now, you might be wondering: why even bother with philosophy? Down here in Georgia, we know that life's big questions don't always come with answers, but asking them is what makes us human. Philosophy matters because it invites us to pause, to see the world not just as it is, but as it could be. It teaches us to savor the good, to learn from the hard, and to grow through it all. It challenges us to look deeper, to seek purpose, and to find clarity.

Philosophy in Action

This chapter will introduce key questions that readers can carry with them:

- *What does it mean to live well?*

- *How do we find meaning amid uncertainty?*

- *What can life's simplest moments teach us about being human?*

A Southern Story: Lessons from the General Store

There's a little general store down the road, the kind of place that smells like fresh peaches in the summer and roasted peanuts in the fall. Miss Giles' runnin' the register most days—silver curls tucked under her visor, sharp as a tack, and sweet as honey. Folks from all over town stop by for their groceries, their gossip, and every now and again, a dose of Miss Giles' wisdom.

I remember one time, a young man stepped in, his shoulders hunched like he'd been carrying the weight of the world. He didn't say much, just grabbed a loaf of bread and a bottle of soda and shuffled up to the counter. Miss Giles studied him for a moment—her eyes twinkling like she knew something he didn't—then asked, "You alright there, son?"

He hesitated. "Just got laid off at the factory," he mumbled. "Don't know how I'm gonna make rent this month."

Now, anyone else might've just rung him up and sent him on his way, but Miss Giles? She reached under the counter and pulled out a slip of paper. "I want you to take this," she said, handing him a flyer for the local job fair. "And while you're at it, take this, too." She slid a bag of peanuts across the counter, smiled, and added, "Things have a way of workin' out, son, even when you don't think they will."

The young man looked at her like he didn't know what to say. Maybe it wasn't much—just a flyer and some peanuts—but in that moment, Miss Giles had done more than make a sale. She'd climbed into his skin, walked around in it, and offered him a little light where there'd been none before.

Reflections on Philosophy

What Miss Giles did that day wasn't just kindness—it was philosophy in action. She understood that life's struggles aren't always visible, and sometimes a little empathy goes a long way. Her gesture was a reminder that we're all walking our own winding paths, and now and then, it's worth pausing to share the journey.

Philosophy doesn't have to be grand or complicated. Sometimes, it's as simple as seeing the world through someone else's eyes, listening to their story, and offering what you can—even if it's just a smile and a bag of peanuts.

A Southern Story: Wisdom from the Old Oak

There's an old oak tree just outside the churchyard in town, its roots twisting deep into the red Georgia clay. Folks say it's been standing there longer than anyone can remember, shading Sunday picnics and quiet conversations for generations. One summer afternoon, I saw old

Mr. Gus sitting beneath it, his straw hat perched low and a whittling knife working steadily on a block of pine.

Now, Mr. Gus wasn't a man of many words. His wisdom came in short phrases, like pieces of a puzzle you had to figure out on your own. That day, a young girl—barely ten and full of sass—came bounding over. She plopped down on the grass beside him and asked, "Why do you sit here all day, Mr. Gus? Don't you ever get bored?"

Without looking up, he said, "Nope. The world's too big to get bored with it."

She frowned. "What do you mean? Ain't nothin' exciting going on here."

He chuckled, a low rumble like distant thunder. "You're lookin' too fast, darlin'. Slow down, and the world'll show you what it's made of."

The girl tilted her head, puzzled, but she stayed quiet and watched as Mr. Gus finished carving the pine into a tiny bird. He handed it to her, smiled, and said, "Every little thing has somethin' to say, if you've got the patience to listen."

Reflections on Philosophy

Mr. Gus wasn't spinning grand theories that day—he was living them. His words and actions echoed the philosophy that understanding starts with slowing down, listening, and appreciating the world for what it is, not just what we expect it to be. It's the same wisdom we find in the works of Laozi, who wrote about harmony with the rhythms of nature, and Emerson, who called for muted observation of life's truths.

In the South, life has a way of teaching you patience—whether it's waiting for peaches to ripen or listening to the cicadas sing their summer songs. And it's that patience, that attentiveness, that opens the door to understanding. Like Mr. Gus, we all have something to learn from the world, if only we take the time to notice it.

Teach Me Patience, Lord

Charles E. Cravey

Teach me patience, Lord, to walk with the earth,
To tread where moss softens stone.
Let me linger in the morning's hush,
Where Your whispers are fully known.

Teach me patience, Lord, in the river's curve,
Its waters unhurried, yet bold.
To learn from its journey, slow and steady,
Its grace shaped by banks that hold.

Teach me patience, Lord, in the oak's rise,
Its roots grasping deep through the clay.
Each year etched in its wide, sturdy rings,
A promise: all blooms in Your way.

Teach me patience, Lord, in the sparrow's pause,
That waits while the storm clouds unfurl.
For even the smallest finds faith in the silence.
Its hymn to the world a soft pearl.

Teach me patience, Lord, in the rhythm of life,
In loss, in growth, in repose.
To see that the seasons, in endless rotations,
Offer lessons in all that life sows.

Let me mute my heart, let me open my hands,
And trust in Your guiding design.
Teach me patience, Lord, in every breath,
That Your time may align with mine.

Opening Our Eyes to Philosophy

As René Descartes once said, *"To live without philosophizing is in truth the same as keeping the eyes closed without attempting to open them."* It's a truth that rings as clear as a church bell on a quiet Southern morning. To live without reflection—without questioning, wondering, and seeking—would be like walking through life with your eyes closed, missing the beauty and wisdom that surrounds us.

Philosophy, when you get right down to it, is a way of opening those eyes. It's the art of looking at the world—not just seeing it, but truly understanding it. It's about pausing long enough to ask the questions that matter: What gives life meaning? How can we live with purpose? What does it mean to be good, to be kind, to be present in a world that's forever rushing past?

Through Descartes' words, we're reminded that philosophy isn't something separate from life—it's woven into every moment, every decision, every thought. It's in the way we slow down to notice the sunrise, or in the way we listen deeply to a friend who needs our understanding. When we philosophize, we're not just opening our eyes to the world; we're opening our hearts to it as well.

A Southern Reflection

Down here in Georgia, we're blessed with plenty of open spaces—fields that stretch wide, skies that seem endless. But the real gift lies not in their vastness, but in the way they invite you to pause and look closely. It's the same with philosophy. Whether it's the wisdom of Descartes or the quiet musings of Miss Giles, the act of philosophizing helps us notice the details—the small moments, the hidden truths—that make life meaningful.

A Southern Story: Storms and Steadfast Souls

There's nothing quite like a summer storm in Georgia—the kind that rolls in unexpectedly, heavy and wild, shaking the windows and soaking the fields in minutes flat. I remember one such storm when I was out visiting Miss Mae, who lived at the edge of town in a house with a tin roof that sang when the rain came. Miss Mae was well into her eighties, quick with a smile, and quicker with wisdom.

When the storm hit, I found her sitting on the porch, rocking slow in her chair as the rain poured and the wind howled. "Miss Mae," I called, running up the steps, "Aren't you afraid of the storm?"

She shook her head and smiled. "Why would I be afraid?" she asked. "Storms come and go. It's the soil underneath that stays."

I didn't understand what she meant at first, but she leaned forward, her eyes shining. "Life's just like this, you know. Sometimes it's calm, sometimes it's wild. But what matters is what's steady—what's rooted deep, like the soil."

Miss May has been a widow for the past forty-two years. She had two children, a boy and a girl, but both preceded her in death. She's had plenty of storms to gain wisdom from!

Philosophical Reflections

Miss Mae's words carry the essence of Stoic philosophy, the kind supported by thinkers like Marcus Aurelius and Seneca. Stoicism teaches us that while we can't control the storms of life—whether they're sudden hardships or unexpected challenges—we can control how we respond. It's about finding steadiness in the chaos, grounding ourselves in what truly matters.

Philosophy, in its simplest form, is the soil that roots us—it's the values we hold dear, the perspectives we cultivate, and the choices we make that shape who we are. Just like Miss Mae said, it's what's steady beneath the surface that helps us weather life's wild moments.

A Reflective Prompt for Readers

Can you think of a storm you've had to face in your own life—something that shook you unexpectedly? What rooted you at the time? What kinds of steady truths or values helped you navigate through it? I would suggest that you write them down and reflect on how they shaped your journey.

The Porch as a Philosophy

Down South, the porch is more than just part of a house—it's a sacred space, a place where time slows and reflections take root. It's where you sit to sip sweet tea, watch the rain fall, and let your thoughts wander like the breeze through the magnolias. And as much as anything else, it's a place where questions are asked and life's mysteries pondered.

Miss Mae's storm gave me a lot to think about—what it means to stay grounded when the winds howl, and why it's worth remembering the things that don't change when everything else does. Sitting on that porch, I realized that philosophy doesn't always come from books or lectures. Sometimes it comes from the steady rhythm of a rocking chair, the sound of rain on a tin roof, or the calm of someone who knows that storms don't last forever.

The Wisdom of Balance

Philosophy often teaches us about balance—between action and reflection, chaos and calm, movement and stillness. The ancient Chinese philosopher Laozi captured this beautifully in the *Tao Te Ching* when he wrote, *"Be still like a mountain and flow like a great river."* That same wisdom is alive and well in Southern life, where patience and adaptability are virtues shaped by long summers, slow-growing crops, and the unpredictability of nature.

Miss Mae's words mirrored this philosophy. To find peace in the chaos, we have to root ourselves in what's steady and learn to flow with what can't be controlled. It's about recognizing that while storms will come, they always pass—and in their wake, the soil remains, ready to nourish new growth.

Inviting Reflection

Here's another prompt for you to help you connect personally with these ideas:

- *Think of your own "porch" moments—the muted spaces in your life where you've had time to reflect. What truths have you discovered there? How have those moments shaped your understanding of what matters most?*

The Porch-Light of Philosophy

Philosophy, in many ways, is like a porch light that stays on long after the sun goes down. It offers a steady glow, guiding us through life's uncertainties and helping us see the world with clarity and warmth. In the South, we know a thing or two about porch lights—how they invite you in when the night feels long and how they remind you that there's always a place to find rest and reflection.

Just like that light, philosophy doesn't always give us answers, but it gives us a way to keep searching. It challenges us to pause, to ponder, and to ask questions—even when the answers feel out of reach. And isn't that what life's about? Finding meaning in the questions, not just the answers?

A Story from the Fields

Let's head into the fields for the next story. Picture this: a farmer stands in the early morning light, boots sinking into the damp soil as he surveys his crops. The rows of green stretch out before him, each plant a testament to patience and hard work. He knows that no amount of rushing will make the harvest come sooner—nature has its own rhythm, and all he can do is tend to it with care and trust.

One day, his neighbor comes by, his hands stained with dirt, and a worry line etched across his brow. "Looks like rain's comin'," he says. "What if it washes the crops clean out?"

The farmer wipes his brow and smiles. "Rain may fall, and storms may roll," he says. "But the roots will hold, as long as we've tended to them right."

Philosophical Insights

The farmer's wisdom echoes the words of Confucius, who taught that life's virtues—patience, humility, diligence—are like the roots of a healthy plant. They're not always visible, but they keep us steady, even when the storms come. Philosophy reminds us that the harvest isn't just about the fruits we see; it's about the care we put into the soil, the roots, and the time we spend nurturing what matters most.

A Reader's Reflection

Let's join the farmer in reflection:

- *Think about the roots of your life—the values and practices that keep you steady. Are there areas you could tend to more carefully? How might philosophy guide your efforts to nurture what matters most?*

A Southern Story: The Empty Chair

There's a diner on Main Street where the coffee's always hot, and the conversations flow like a winding river. In the corner booth, there's an empty chair that everyone seems to leave untouched. It used to belong to a man named Mr. Roy, who came in every morning like clockwork—hat tipped low, newspaper in hand, always with a kind word for whoever passed by.

Mr. Roy was known for asking questions, the kind that made you stop and think: "What's been the best part of your day so far?" or "If today was your last, how would you spend it?" Simple questions, but they had a way of staying with you, like the aftertaste of a good cup of coffee.

One day, Mr. Roy didn't come in. Folks later learned he'd passed quietly at home, his life lived fully and without regret. But even now, that empty chair in the corner seems to whisper his questions, reminding anyone who sits nearby to reflect, to connect, and to live with intention.

Philosophical Reflections

Mr. Roy's questions mirror the teachings of Socrates, who believed that "the unexamined life is not worth living." Philosophy isn't about having all the answers—it's about daring to ask the questions that matter. Through his gentle inquiries, Mr. Roy invited those around him to pause and consider their lives in a deeper way.

In the hustle of daily living, it's easy to overlook the small moments that make life meaningful. Philosophy challenges us to reclaim those moments, to slow down and savor the warmth of a morning coffee or the wisdom of a thoughtful question. Just like Mr. Roy's empty chair, it reminds us that every moment is an opportunity to reflect and grow.

A Reader's Reflection

To carry Mr. Roy's spirit forward, here are more prompts for you:

- *Think of a question that has stayed with you—one that made you stop and reflect. How did it change your perspective? If you could ask yourself one meaningful question every day, what would it be?*

A Southern Story: The River's Lesson

There's a stretch of river down near the edge of town, where the water runs clear and quiet, winding lazily through the pines. Old Mr. Caleb used to fish there every Saturday morning, his tackle box balanced on the bank and a pipe resting in the corner of his mouth. Caleb wasn't in it for the fish, though; he rarely brought any home. "The fish are just an excuse," he'd say, chuckling. "What I'm after is the waiting."

One morning, as I sat beside him, the line tugged—a real bite this time. Caleb smiled, reeled it in, and held the fish for a moment before carefully releasing it back into the water. "Why'd you let it go?" I asked.

He tapped his pipe and leaned back against the bank. "It's not about catching, son," he said. "It's about being here—listening to the river, feeling the breeze, knowing that there's more to life than what's right in front of ya."

Philosophical Reflections

Mr. Caleb's muted wisdom echoes the philosophy of mindfulness—living in the moment and appreciating the simplicity of being. It's a lesson shared by Thoreau, who sought solitude at Walden Pond to understand the essence of life, and Buddha, who taught that presence brings peace. Caleb's fishing wasn't about the fish; it was about finding harmony with the river, with nature, and with the muted spaces in between.

Philosophy reminds us that life isn't just about outcomes—it's about experiences, the moments that invite us to pause and reflect. Like the river, life flows with a rhythm that's both constant and ever-changing, and the key to understanding it lies in taking the time to listen.

A Reader's Reflection

To connect this lesson with your journey, here's a prompt:

- *Think of a "river moment" in your life—a time when you savored the simplicity of the present. What did it teach you about yourself, and how can you bring that lesson into your daily life?*

The Eagle and the Echo of Presence

Years ago, on a muted morning at the North Georgia Toccoa River, I shared a fishing trip with my son, Jonathan—a day meant to be nothing more than casting lines and sharing small talk, the kind of moment that doesn't ask much from life, except for a little peace. The river was calm, its waters winding gently through the hills like liquid silver. Jonathan was fishing upstream, his focus locked on the ripples and shadows, waiting for a rainbow trout to bite. I was farther downriver, sitting on the bank, letting the cool breeze carry away any thoughts that didn't belong in the stillness.

And then it happened.

Out of the sky, as if conjured by the river itself, a bald eagle swept down before me. Its wings were broad, its feathers gleaming against the sunlight. With perfect precision, it pierced the water and rose, clutching a rainbow trout—a shimmering prize—within its talons. For a moment, time seemed to stop. The eagle soared, its silhouette reflected in the river's glassy surface, and then it disappeared downstream, leaving me awestruck and silent.

When I called to Jonathan to see if he'd witnessed it, he shook his head, still intent on his fishing. "What eagle?" he asked, unaware that such a moment had just passed him by.

The Lesson of the River

That eagle, in all its beauty and power, taught me something I've carried ever since: Life offers us these moments—rare, breathtaking, unrepeatable—but only if we're paying attention. It's so easy to miss them, caught up in the smaller distractions we cling to, like fishing lines in the current. Philosophy teaches us that presence—the act of truly seeing, hearing, and feeling—is the key to catching life's treasures before they take flight.

Jonathan didn't see the eagle. And how often do we miss our own? How often does the world give us glimpses of something extraordinary, only for us to be too busy, too distracted, to notice? The river, the eagle—they remind us to pause, to open our eyes, and to embrace the simple and profound beauty that surrounds us every day.

A Reader's Reflection

Let me invite you to reflect on this profound lesson:

- *Think about when life gifted you something extraordinary—something you almost missed, or perhaps missed. What distracted you, and how might presence help you embrace these moments in the future?*

A Southern Story: Lessons from the Candle Shop

There's a small candle shop tucked away in the square's corner, where the windows are always fogged with the sweet scent of beeswax and lavender. It's run by Miss Lucille, a soft-spoken woman whose hands are always steady as she pours wax into molds and trims wicks with precision. Folks say her candles burn brighter and longer than anyone's, though Miss Lucille will tell you it isn't just about the wax or the wick. "It's the pouring that makes the difference," she once said to me, "how patient you are with the heat, how careful you are with the flow."

One rainy afternoon, as I watched her work, I asked why she chose such a muted craft—why not something faster, louder, more exciting?

She smiled, her eyes soft with understanding. "The way I see it," she said, "life's a lot like a candle. If you rush the pouring, the flame will flicker and fade. But if you take your time, if you give it care, the light you make will last."

Philosophical Reflections

Miss Lucille's gentle wisdom echoes Aristotle's philosophy of virtue and balance. Just as a candle must be poured with patience and care, Aristotle believed that a good life is crafted through deliberate choices and steady practice. Virtue, he taught, lies in the middle ground—between excess and deficiency—and it's through small, consistent actions that we build a life worth illuminating.

In the Southern cadence of Miss Lucille's words, we hear a timeless truth: Life isn't about rushing to the finish; it's about savoring the process, pouring each moment with the care it deserves. Philosophy reminds us that, while the outcome may be important, the journey matters just as much. It's in the pouring that the flame finds its strength.

A Reader's Reflection

Here's a prompt from Miss Lucille's lesson:

- *Think about a "pouring moment" in your life—a time when patience and care shaped the outcome. What did it teach you about the importance of process over result? How can you bring more deliberate attention to your daily tasks?*

A Southern Story: The Patchwork Quilt

Down in the county's heart, Miss Myrtle's house is known for two things: her apple pie and her quilts. Her quilts aren't just blankets—they're works of art, stitched together from scraps of old fabric, each piece holding a memory. There's the patch from her husband's Sunday shirt, the corner from her daughter's first dress, the square from her son's army uniform.

One afternoon, as she worked on a new quilt, I asked her why she used such mismatched scraps instead of buying new fabric. She paused, holding up a piece of faded gingham. "This fabric's got a story," she said. "Every stitch brings it back to life. New cloth's got no story yet."

As her hands moved over the quilt, her eyes softened. "Life's just like this quilt," she said. "It ain't perfect, but it's the imperfections that give it character. Every tear, every patch, every mismatched piece—together, they make something whole."

Philosophical Reflections

Miss Myrtle's quilt holds the same wisdom as Marcus Aurelius' *Meditations*. The Stoic philosopher believed that life's challenges and imperfections aren't obstacles—they're part of the design woven into the fabric of our experiences. He wrote, *"The impediment to action advances action. What stands in the way becomes the way."* In other words, it's through embracing life's flaws that we find its beauty and strength.

Miss Myrtle's patchwork quilt reminds us that life's imperfections don't diminish its value—they enrich it. Philosophy teaches us to see our own struggles and scars as pieces of a greater whole, stitched together to create something uniquely our own.

A Reader's Reflection

Here's another prompt for you to consider:

- *Think of a "patchwork" in your life—a challenge or imperfection that's become part of your story. How has it shaped you? What lessons has it added to your personal quilt?*

A Southern Story: The Weeping Willow

At the edge of a neighbor's farm stood a weeping willow tree, its branches dipping low as though they were bowing to the earth. Folks around town said the tree had been there for generations, surviving floods, droughts, and storms that flattened barns and scattered fields. It stood quiet and unassuming, offering shade to anyone who needed to rest.

One summer afternoon, as I passed by the farm, I noticed old Mr. Jim sitting beneath the willow, his straw hat tipped forward and his hands folded in thought. I joined him, and as we sat together, the soft rustle of the leaves whispered like secrets being shared. "How's it that this old tree has outlasted so many storms?" I asked.

Mr. Jim tilted his hat back and looked up at the tree, a small smile on his face. "It bends, son," he said. "When the winds blow strong, it don't fight back. It just bows low and waits for the storm to pass. Most trees, they snap because they try to stand too stiff. But this willow? It knows how to survive."

Philosophical Reflections

The weeping willow's muted strength embodies the wisdom of Laozi in the *Tao Te Ching*: *"The soft overcomes the hard."* Laozi taught that flexibility and adaptability are among the greatest virtues in life. Like the willow, we find resilience not in resisting life's challenges, but in bending with them—learning to adapt, endure, and grow stronger.

Philosophy reminds us that persistence doesn't always mean standing tall. Sometimes, it means bowing gracefully, weathering the storm, and rising again when the winds have settled. The willow teaches us the power of humility, patience, and trust in life's rhythms.

A Reader's Reflection

To connect the weeping willow's lesson with your experience, here's this prompt:

- *Think about a storm in your life—a challenge that felt overwhelming. May I ask if you resisted it, or did you bend with it? What did the experience teach you about perseverance and adaptability?*

A Southern Story: The Hands that Persevere

When my pastor entrusted me with visiting the residents of a nursing facility, I thought of it as a duty—an opportunity to bring comfort, to listen, to give. What I didn't expect was to be brought face-to-face with my own past, wrapped in the figure of a man who had once been my mentor and counselor during my time at Georgia Southern University in the 1970s.

As I entered his room, recognition crossed both our faces like sunlight breaking through clouds. Though the years had worn him, etched lines on his skin and slowed his movement, his spirit remained steadfast. We spoke for a while, and he shared his struggles—a failing body, the steady grief of losing his beloved wife, and the muted determination to keep going, day by day. When he gripped my hand as we prayed together, his strength felt like an echo of the man who had guided me decades ago—a reminder that while time may take its toll, the essence of perseverance is timeless.

Philosophical Reflections

This encounter holds a mirror to the philosophy of time and change, echoed in the words of Søren Kierkegaard: *"Life can only* be understood *backwards, but it must be lived forwards."* It's a truth that gently reminds us of the interplay between memory and presence. Seeing my mentor was a bittersweet reflection of both the man he was and the man he is—a realization that we cannot return to the past, but we can honor it by cherishing the bonds that endure through the years.

There's also the philosophy of resilience—of facing the inevitability of change with grace and determination. My mentor's words, *"I still manage to make it day-by-day,"* echo the wisdom of Viktor Frankl, who wrote of finding meaning in life's challenges. Perseverance isn't about denying hardship; it's about embracing it with a spirit that refuses to falter.

The Lesson of Presence

As I sat with my mentor, I couldn't help but wish for the man he had been in our Sociology classes years ago. But the gift of the moment lay not in wishing, but in seeing—truly seeing the man before me, not as he was, but as he is. That prayer, his firm grip on my hand, was a bridge between then and now, a testament to the strength that endures even as the body grows weaker. It's a lesson in presence—in accepting life's ebb and flow and finding gratitude for what remains.

A Reader's Reflection

This story holds a profound lesson for us:

- *Think of someone who has shaped your life—a mentor, a friend,*

*a loved one. How have they changed over time, and how have
you changed in return? What moments have reminded you to
embrace them as they are, while cherishing who they've been?*

A Southern Story: Hitting Life's Curve Balls

There was a time when I had the privilege of serving as the pastor
to a remarkable congregation, and among its members was a man I'll
never forget—Stiles Stevens. At seventy-five years old, Stiles wasn't a
man to let life's challenges slow him down. Every Sunday, despite the
burdens he quietly carried—both a Colostomy bag and an Ileostomy
bag that required careful attention before he could even step out the
door—there he was, front and center, faithfully waiting for the morn-
ing service.

It wasn't just his presence that stood out, though it inspired every-
one who saw him. It was the steadfast joy in his voice and the muted
wisdom he shared when he said, "Pastor, life has a way of throwing us
curve balls, but if we learn to read them with keen eyes, we can gauge
them before they make it to the plate and hit a homer. I've had a few
curve balls in my life that I couldn't quite hit, but I've still made it."

Stiles' words remind me of Babe Ruth's famous quote: *"Every strike
brings me closer to the next home run."* Ruth, like Stiles, understood
that perseverance isn't about avoiding failure—it's about embracing
it as part of the journey. Each missed swing, each curve ball, is a step
closer to when everything aligns and the bat connects with the ball,
sending it soaring.

Philosophical Reflections

Stiles' life was a living example of resilience, a lesson echoed in the
teachings of the Stoics. Seneca once said, *"A gem cannot be polished*

without friction, nor a man perfected without trials." Stiles' ability to face life's challenges with grace and humor wasn't about avoiding difficulty—it was about confronting it with courage and determination, knowing that even the missed curve balls are part of the game.

Philosophy teaches us that resilience isn't just about enduring—it's about finding meaning in the struggle. Stiles didn't let his physical hardships define him; instead, he focused on showing up, on participating fully in the life he was given, and on embracing the opportunities he could still reach. His metaphor of hitting curve balls reminds us that even when we don't hit a homer, the act of standing at the plate—ready, willing, and hopeful—is itself a victory.

The Lesson of Faith and Dedication

What stands out most about Stiles is his unwavering faith—the kind of faith that gets you up on a Sunday morning, no matter the effort it takes, because you know there's something greater waiting for you. His presence in the pew wasn't just an act of habit; it was a declaration of hope, of devotion, of gratitude for the life he still lived. His faith wasn't passive; it was active, resilient, and inspiring to everyone blessed to witness it.

A Reader's Reflection

Here's a prompt for you to engage with Stiles' story:

- *Think of a time when life threw you a curve ball—one that seemed impossible to hit. How did you respond? What kept you standing at the plate, and what lessons did you take from the experience?*

A Southern Story: The Cricket's Song

There's a dirt road just outside of town that winds its way through fields of wildflowers and past a rickety old fence marking the edge of what used to be the Lunsford family farm. The house is gone now, but the porch swing still hangs from a lone pecan tree, swaying gently in the breeze, even without anyone there to push it. It was on that swing, many years ago, that I first sat with Miss Nelly Lunsford, a woman whose heart was as big as the Georgia sky.

Miss Nelly had a way of making you feel like you belonged, no matter who you were or where you came from. She spoke with a softness that made you lean in, not wanting to miss a word, and she had a story for every occasion. One summer evening, as the crickets began their song and the fireflies blinked along the fence line, she shared a piece of wisdom I'll never forget.

"Life's a lot like these crickets," she said, her voice a soft melody. "You don't notice 'em in the day, when the world's too loud. But when the noise settles and the light fades, that's when their song comes alive. It's the quiet moments, child—the ones folks don't pay much mind to—that end up meaning the most."

Philosophical Reflections

Miss Nelly's words remind me of Ralph Waldo Emerson's call to embrace the quiet truths of life. He wrote, *"To the attentive eye, each moment of the year has its own beauty, and in the same field, it beholds, every hour, a picture which was never seen before, and which shall never be seen again."* Both Emerson and Miss Nelly understood that the beauty of life doesn't shout—it whispers. It waits for us to slow down, to listen, to find meaning in the stillness.

In the South, where time seems to linger and the nights stretch long, there's a unique opportunity to notice the moments that might otherwise be lost—the cricket's song, the sway of an old porch swing, the glow of fireflies. Philosophy teaches us that these moments are the essence of life's poetry, subtle and fleeting, yet profoundly rich.

The Lesson of Attentiveness

Miss Nelly's wisdom is a reminder to step back from the rush and let the world come into focus. It's about learning to quiet the noise, to let the light fade just enough to see what truly matters. It's in these moments—the small, unnoticed spaces—that we find the heart of life.

A Reader's Reflection

I invite you into this gentle reflection. Let me include this prompt:

- *Think of a time when you slowed down and noticed something you might have otherwise missed—a sound, a feeling, a fleeting moment of beauty. How did it change your perspective, and how can you create more space for these moments in your life?*

A Southern Story: The Ripple of Connection

Late evenings in our home often carry a muted rhythm—the hum of the ceiling fan, the glow of a lamp, and the soft rustling of pages as my wife and I unwind with books in hand. But the other night, as the hour grew late, she let out a yawn—a deep, unhurried sigh of weariness—and without even realizing it, I yawned along with her. It happened so quickly, so reflexively, as if her breath had carried something invisible but undeniable straight to me.

It was such a simple moment, but as I reflected on it, I realized how often we mirror one another in ways that go far beyond yawns. A smile shared across a room sparks another, the sound of laughter echoes like a melody, and even unspoken emotions—joy, frustration, tenderness—ripple through the spaces between us. John Donne captured this truth centuries ago when he wrote, *"No man is an island, entire of itself; every man is a piece of* the *continent, a part of the main."* His words remind us we are all connected, not as isolated individuals, but as threads in the fabric of humanity.

Philosophical Reflections

My experience reflects the concept of interconnectedness, a theme explored by philosophers like Martin Buber and John Donne. Donne's observation reminds us that our lives are interconnected; each of our actions—yawns, smiles, or kind words—creates ripples affecting others in ways we may never fully grasp. It's a call to recognize the shared humanity that binds us, to see ourselves not as islands, but as integral parts of a greater whole.

This interconnectedness also ties into the scientific principle of "contagious behavior." Yawning, in particular, is highly contagious, partly because it activates empathy within us. It's a biological reminder that we are social creatures, wired to respond to and reflect the emotions and actions of others.

The Ripple Effect in Life

Just like my shared yawn, this idea carries over into other aspects of life—the way a kind word can uplift someone's spirits, or the way frustration can spread if we let it. It's a reminder that our actions, even the smallest ones, don't exist in isolation. They create ripples, shaping the environments we inhabit and the relationships we hold dear.

In the South, where community and connection are at the heart of life, this ripple effect feels especially meaningful. A neighbor's wave can brighten the day, a shared meal can mend fences, and a church pew full of hymns can fill the soul. These moments show us how deeply we affect one another, often without realizing it.

A Reader's Reflection

Here's a prompt to further your journey:

- *Think about when you instinctively responded to someone else's action—a smile, a laugh, a gesture. What did it teach you about the ways we influence one another, and how can you create more positive ripples in your daily life?*

A Southern Story: The Wash of Renewal

Down here, there's something sacred about the ritual of bathing, especially after a long, humid day in Georgia, when the dirt clings to your skin like it's got nowhere better to go. Stepping into the cool water, letting it rush over you, feels like letting the day slip away—a reset, a chance to leave behind what no longer serves you and come out feeling fresh, ready to face what's next.

Science tells us that every time we bathe, our bodies shed millions of epithelial cells—tiny pieces of ourselves that we don't need anymore, washed away in the flow. But as I think about it, there's more to it than just biology. It feels like there's a lesson in there somewhere—a reminder that just like our bodies let go of the old to make room for the new; we have to do the same with our lives. We have to learn to release the burdens, the fears, the moments that weigh us down, and trust in our ability to renew.

Philosophical Reflections

This ritual of shedding and renewing brings to mind Heraclitus' wisdom: *"No man ever steps in the same river twice, for it's not the same river and he's not the same man."* The river, always flowing, teaches us that change is constant, and our lives—like those epithelial cells—are made for moving forward. We're not meant to hold on to yesterday's dust, but to let it wash away so we can face tomorrow with a lighter heart.

Here in the South, the image of cleansing has an even deeper meaning. Think about baptism, the sacred act of stepping into the water to mark a fresh beginning. It's not just about washing the physical—it's about renewing the soul, leaving behind the shadows, and stepping into the sunlight. It's the belief that no matter where you've been, there's always room to rise anew.

The Lesson of Renewal

So often in life, we carry burdens that cling to us, refusing to let go. But the body, in its muted wisdom, shows us how to shed the weight and trust in the process of renewal. It's not about forgetting—those burdens may leave marks like the day's dust on your skin—but it's about letting go enough to make room for growth. Every time we bathe, we're reminded of this simple truth: To move forward, we have to release what holds us back.

A Reader's Reflection

Here's a moment of pause:

- *Think of something in your life you've struggled to let go of—a fear, a regret, or a moment that clings to you like the day's dust. How might the act of renewal, like the shedding of cells, help you release it and move forward with lighter steps?*

A Southern Story: The Oak Tree's Shadow

In the corner of our yard, there's an old oak tree that's been there longer than I have. Its branches stretch wide, casting a lace of shadows across the earth below, and in the spring, it pushes out new leaves with the delicate beauty that makes you stop and catch your breath. It's the kind of tree that holds memories—picnics on its roots, laughter beneath its shade, even whispered prayers in the quiet of its shadow. But as much as it stands,it also changes. Every season brings something new—new leaves in April, a canopy of green by June, and bare branches stretching toward the sky come November.

One day, as I sat beneath its branches, watching the shadows shift in the afternoon sun, I thought about all the years it had weathered—the winds, the rains, the seasons that shaped it. And yet, here it stands, rooted and resilient, quietly doing what trees do best: growing, adapting, and providing for those lucky enough to sit beneath its shade.

Philosophical Reflections

The oak's steady rhythm of growth mirrors the philosophy of the seasons, embraced by thinkers like Marcus Aurelius in his *Meditations*. He wrote, *"Accept the things to which fate binds you, and love the people with whom fate brings you together, but do so with all your heart."* The oak, rooted deeply yet flexible in its branches, teaches us the beauty of acceptance—the idea that life is ever-changing, and each season brings its own challenges and blessings.

In its Southern simplicity, the oak also reminds me of Wendell Berry's words: *"The Earth is what we all have in common."* Like the tree's shadow, we all cast something into the world—something that lingers, that provides comfort, which reaches others in ways we may never fully understand.

The Lesson of Quiet Strength

That old oak teaches us to embrace change while staying rooted in what matters. It invites us to weather the seasons of life with muted strength, trusting that even in moments of bare branches and empty skies, the verdant leaves will return. And it reminds us that sometimes, the most profound impact isn't loud—it's muted, subtle, woven into the shade we offer to others.

A Reader's Reflection

Let me encourage you to reflect on your own seasons:
- *Think of a time when life brought change—a season of growth, loss, or renewal. How did you stay rooted through it all, and what shadows did you cast that reached others?*

A Southern Story: The Tent Chronicles

It was a few years back, during one of those long summer weekends when the North Georgia Mountains beckon with the promise of escape. My wife and I found ourselves at a popular campsite, surrounded by the whispering pines and the smell of campfire smoke—a little slice of Southern heaven. We'd already pitched our tent and were taking a stroll through the camping area, soaking in the scenery, when we stumbled upon a scene that was all too familiar to anyone who's spent time in the South.

There he was—a man kneeling beside his tent, poles sprawled across the ground like puzzle pieces that refused to fit. His face was a mix of determination and frustration, a man on a mission to conquer what he saw as a simple task. Because, in the South, pride runs deep, and figuring out how to put up a tent without consulting the instructions is practically a rite of passage. After all, we Southern men "know" how to do everything—or at least, that's what we tell ourselves. Asking for help, especially from a manual, just doesn't sit well with the spirit of self-reliance.

But as his frustration grew, and the tent remained flat, my wife stepped in. Quietly, without fanfare, she picked up the instruction manual, began sorting the poles, and put them together with the efficiency of someone who sees a problem and fixes it without hesitation. The tent rose before his eyes, sturdy and upright, ready to serve as a home for his family's adventure.

As she finished, he looked up at her and said, "I appreciate it, but I would have sooner or later figured out how to do it." His tone was kind but firm—his pride intact, even as he accepted her help.

Reflections on Southern Pride

This moment, as simple as it seemed, holds a mirror to the South's unique blend of self-reliance and quiet community. There's a pride in doing things on your own, in solving problems with grit and ingenuity, but there's also a beauty in knowing when to accept a helping hand—even if it comes with a gentle reminder that instructions have their purpose.

Philosophically, it resonates with the idea of humility—a virtue praised by thinkers like Confucius, who taught, *"Humility is the solid foundation of all virtues."* The Southern spirit, as proud as it is, teaches us that while independence is admirable, there's strength in recognizing the value of collaboration. The man's reluctance to rely on the manual is a reflection of pride, but his acceptance of help reminds us that growth often requires us to let go of stubbornness and embrace the wisdom others bring.

The Lesson in Connection

There's an undeniable charm in the quirks of Southern culture, but this story also carries a deeper lesson: that connection often happens in the simplest of moments. My wife's willingness to step in, his gratitude despite his pride—these small acts of kindness and resilience weave the fabric of community. Life in the South is full of these moments, where pride, humor, and humanity come together in ways that leave us smiling long after the tent poles are packed away.

A Reader's Reflection

I invite you into this story with the following question:

- *Think of when pride led you to tackle something on your own. How did you respond when someone stepped in to help? What did the experience teach you about humility and the value of teamwork?*

A Southern Story: The Whittler's Bench

Down in the square of a small Southern town, there used to be a long wooden bench that sat beneath an old oak tree. It was nothing fancy—just a sturdy plank with legs weathered gray by time—but to the folks who gathered there, it was more than a bench. It was the Whittler's Bench, where men would sit with pocketknives in hand, carving away at bits of cedar or pine, their hands moving as if they carried the stories of generations.

The whittlers weren't in a hurry, and they weren't trying to make anything perfect. A few carved birds, some whittled pipes, and others just whittled for the sake of it, letting the shavings pile up at their feet. What mattered wasn't the outcome; it was the act of doing—of sitting together, talking about the weather, the crops, the world beyond the square, and occasionally falling into a muted rhythm where no words were needed.

One old timer, Mr. Willis, who seemed to know more about life than anyone, used to say, "Whittlin' ain't about finishin'; it's about what you learn while your hands are busy."

Philosophical Reflections

Mr. Willis' wisdom speaks to the philosophy of process over outcome, a theme echoed by thinkers like Laozi in the *Tao Te Ching*: "A journey *of a thousand miles begins with a single step.*" Whittling, like life, isn't a race to the finish—it's an opportunity to be present, to reflect, and to connect. The process itself carries meaning, shaping not just the wood but the whittler too.

The Whittler's Bench also represents community. In a world that often rushes toward goals, it's a reminder that slowing down and sharing a quiet moment with others is as important as anything we might accomplish. Philosophy teaches us that these simple acts of being and belonging are the foundation of a meaningful life.

The Lesson of Presence

The art of whittling reminds us to find value in the act of doing, rather than fixating on the result. Whether it's carving wood, planting seeds, or having a heartfelt conversation, the process is where life happens. The bench, the oak tree, the steady hands of the whittlers—they're all a call to slow down, to live intentionally, and to cherish the quiet beauty of the moment.

A Reader's Reflection

I encourage you to take this lesson to heart and let's include this prompt:

- *Think of something in your life that allows you to slow down—a hobby, a tradition, or even a quiet moment. How does the act of doing enrich your experience, and how can you embrace the process more fully?*

A Southern Story: The Pie on the Porch

There's a tradition in the South that doesn't need explaining—it's a language spoken in casseroles and pies, in mason jars filled with sweet tea and kindness. Folks here know that when times get tough, it's not about grand gestures—it's about showing up, often with something homemade and heartfelt in hand.

I remember a summer not too long ago, when Mrs. Clara Jenkins, who lived just down the road, lost her husband after sixty years of marriage. Her house, once lively with the hum of shared memories, fell into a muted stillness that tugged at everyone in the neighborhood. Without a word or a plan, the community began its unspoken ritual.

The front porch steps of Mrs. Jenkins' house became the gathering place for pies, cakes, and casseroles—a tapestry of comfort wrapped in foil and handwritten notes.

The pie on the porch wasn't just about feeding her—it was about reminding her she wasn't alone. It was about saying, "We're here," in the muted way Southerners often do, with actions that speak louder than words. Overtime, as the porch overflowed with dishes and the house filled with familiar voices, the stillness lifted. Life moved forward, gently, like the steady swing of her rocking chair.

Philosophical Reflections

This tradition embodies the philosophy of shared humanity—a theme explored by thinkers like Maya Angelou, who wrote, *"We are more alike than we are unalike."* In the South, these acts of kindness remind us of our interconnectedness—the idea that we are never truly alone because we belong to something greater than ourselves.

It also ties into Aristotle's belief in the importance of friendship and community as the foundation of a good life. Aristotle argued humans are social beings, designed not to exist in isolation but to thrive in companionship. The pie on the porch is more than just a kind act—it's the physical manifestation of that truth, a reminder that community sustains us in life's hardest moments.

The Lesson of Connection

This story teaches us that connection isn't always about grand gestures or eloquent speeches. Sometimes, it's about showing up, about the steady rhythm of small acts of kindness that say, "You matter." It's about knowing that when life gets heavy, a pie on the porch can mean the world.

A Reader's Reflection

Let me offer you a moment of pause to reflect on your own communities:

- *Think of a time when someone showed up for you—a kind act that reminded you of the strength of connection. How can you pay that forward in your own life and community?*

Building Momentum: The Tapestry of Community

The pie on the porch is just one thread in the larger tapestry of Southern life, where connection often comes in the form of muted gestures that speak volumes. Whether it's lending a hand to a neighbor wrestling with tent poles or sitting with an old mentor to pray, these moments remind us of the unspoken bonds that hold us together. In the South, pride and humility dance together—there's a strength in tackling life's challenges, but there's an even greater strength in knowing when to let others in.

As Chapter One unfolds, we see a pattern emerge—a reflection on the ways we navigate life's storms, renew ourselves, and lean on the people around us. From the steadfast presence of Stiles Stevens to the whittlers carving wisdom into wood, the common thread is connection. It's the idea that resilience isn't just about standing alone—it's about the hands that steady us, the voices that comfort us, and the shared understanding that together, we can weather anything.

Philosophical and Spiritual Ties

Let me give you a broader philosophical perspective. Let's weave in some timeless wisdom:

- **Maya Angelou's reminder of shared humanity:** *"We are more alike than we are unalike."* Southern life often embodies this truth, bringing people together over shared meals and shared burdens, reminding us of the ties that bind.

- **Kahlil Gibran's thoughts on friendship:** *"And let there be no purpose in friendship save the deepening of the spirit."* Just as a pie on the porch deepens the bond between neighbors, our shared experiences enrich and strengthen our lives.

- **Scriptural reflections:** The Bible speaks often of loving one's neighbor and bearing one another's burdens—principles that shine brightly in the unspoken rituals of the Southern community.

These perspectives reinforce this chapter's themes, grounding them in universal truths that resonate across time and place.

A Hopeful Closing Reflection

As we approach the end of Chapter One, it's time to offer you a moment of hope—an invitation to carry these lessons forward:

"The stories of Stiles Stevens, Miss Myrtle's patchwork quilt, the pie on the porch—all these moments show us that life is as much about connection as it is about perseverance. It's in the shadows we cast, the hands we lend, and the muted *spaces we share that life finds its richest meaning. And as we step forward into the next chapter, let us carry these lessons with us—finding strength in community, grace in resilience, and hope in the enduring spirit of togetherness."*

Reader Engagement

Let me leave you with one final question to ponder:

- *How can you bring these lessons of connection into your own life? Think of one small act of kindness or community you can share today. How might it ripple outward to create something greater?*

2

The Roads That Carry Us

❦

The car hummed along the winding road, the low-hanging branches of magnolias framing the way like nature's cathedral. My wife and I weren't in a hurry; these back roads had a way of making time stretch, of inviting you to linger. Out here, with no destination in mind, the journey itself was the point—and every turn in the road brought a new story, a new lesson, waiting to unfold.

As we drove, a thought crossed my mind: *How many roads have we traveled to get here, not just in miles but in moments?* Life has its way of weaving paths together, some chosen, others unexpected, but all leading us to where we stand today. In the South, the roads themselves seem to tell stories—the cracked pavement, the whisper of pine needles brushing the ground, the distant sound of a whippoorwill calling out into the dusk. They remind us that every journey has meaning, even if the destination isn't yet clear.

The Crossroads Moment

One such road comes to mind—a crossroads moment that changed everything. It was years ago, back when the days felt fuller, and time had yet to carve its lines into my face. There I stood, faced with a decision that would shape my future. It wasn't a simple choice; the path ahead was uncertain, and both roads promised an equal measure of risk and reward. But as Southern wisdom often tells us, *"You've gotta pick a path and walk it—because standing still won't get you anywhere."*

I chose a road, not knowing where it would lead, and looking back now, I can see how it carried me to places I never expected—some filled with joy, others with challenges, but all part of the journey that brought me here.

Nature's Lessons Along the Way

The roads of the South aren't just paved with asphalt; they're lined with lessons. Take the rivers, for example, winding and flowing through valleys and woods. They remind us to be patient, to let life move at its own rhythm instead of rushing to outrun it. The mountains teach us about perspective—the way climbing higher lets us see farther, understanding our place in the larger picture. Even the open fields, stretching out under the sky, teach us about possibility and the endless expanse of what's yet to come.

Philosophical Undertones

This chapter invites us to consider the wisdom of poets and philosophers who've pondered life's roads. Robert Frost's *The Road Not Taken* tells us of the lasting impact our choices make, while Southern literary voices like Flannery O'Connor challenge us to think about the roads we take in terms of faith, morality, and destiny. These reflections give depth to the narrative, grounding it in timeless truths that resonate far beyond the South.

Reader Engagement

To pull you into this journey, let me leave you with a moment to reflect.

- *Think of a road that shaped your life—not just in miles, but in meaning. How did it change you, and how can you carry its lessons forward as you walk the paths ahead?*

The Road Beneath the Arbor

Charles E. Cravey

The road winds softly through pine and field,
Where shadows stretch and secrets yield.
Each turn a whisper, each bend a sigh,
Of lives once lived and dreams gone by.

Beneath the brush, where stories meet,
Her feet once danced in a barefoot beat.
The arbor sang of faith and grace,
Its echoes lingering, a sacred place.

The hearse moves slow, the tires hum.
A journey taken, a life undone.
Yet on this path, her love remains,
In whispered winds, in soft refrains.

The dogwoods bloom, their petals white,
Like prayers that rise into the night.
The mountain watches, the river flows,
And through it all, the memory grows.

For every road must one day end,

Its stories passed from hand to friend.

But even when the miles are through,

The roads we've walked still carry you.

The Old Familiar Road

There are some roads you travel that hold more than just miles—they carry memories, etched into every turn and landmark. On the day of my mother's funeral, we followed the hearse down one such road. It wasn't just the route to her final resting place; it was a passage through the landscapes of her life, a journey steeped in stories she had shared with me as a child and a teen.

As the procession moved, I couldn't help but notice the places that had shaped her—places she had pointed out to me in her gentle, familiar voice. There was the field where she and her siblings had played as children, their laughter carried by the wind. The old church steeple peeked through the trees, the same steeple where she had sung hymns as a young girl, her faith growing with every note. And then, as we turned the last bend, there it was—the cemetery nestled across the road from the old brush arbor campground, a place she had loved with all her heart.

The brush arbor, she once told me, was more than just a gathering spot; it was a sacred space where faith and community intertwined. As children, they'd run barefoot in the grass, their hearts light with the joy of revival meetings, while the elders sang and preached beneath the shelter of the arbor. For her, this wasn't just a resting place—it was home, a place where the roots of her life and her spirit ran deep.

Reflections on Memory and Place

This journey down the old familiar road reminds us of the way places carry meaning—not just for the landmarks themselves, but for the stories and emotions we attach to them. The philosopher Gaston Bachelard once wrote, *"The house shelters daydreaming, the house protects the dreamer, the house allows one to dream in peace."* The places along this road were like a house for my mother's soul, sheltering her memories and allowing her to share them with me, leaving a legacy that lingers long after the road ends.

This story also reminds me of the Southern connection to place—how land, community, and faith become intertwined with identity. In the South, roads don't just take us somewhere; they connect us to who we are and where we come from. They're a part of our story, and in traveling them, we honor the lives and the love that shaped us.

The Lesson of Walking the Road

As we pulled into the cemetery that day, I felt the weight of both grief and gratitude. My mother's last journey wasn't just a procession; it was a tapestry of moments, memories, and meaning. These roads—paths where the past meets the present—remind us that life comprises journeys in which we carry the stories of our ancestors and find strength to move forward, cherishing their love.

A Reader's Reflection

Here's a reflective prompt:

- *Think of a road that holds memories for you—a place tied to someone you loved or a moment that shaped you. What does that road teach you about the connection between place and memory?*

A Southern Story: Georgia Ice Cream

If the South had a signature dish, it would be grits—smooth, comforting, and perfectly unassuming, yet deeply cherished. For many, grits aren't just a food; they're a tradition, a memory, a reminder of what it means to gather around the kitchen table and share love served in a pot. And no one made them quite like my mother. Her cheese grits, lovingly dubbed "Georgia Ice-cream," were the kind of dish that could turn an ordinary breakfast into an event, filling the house with the scent of melted cheese and a warmth that seemed to linger long after the plates were cleared.

There was something magical about watching her make them. She'd stand at the stove, stirring the pot with the precision of someone who didn't need a recipe—she'd memorized the dance of ingredients long ago. Butter, milk, cheese, salt—each added in perfect measure, creating a symphony of flavor that could only come from generations of Southern wisdom. As she stirred, she'd talk—sometimes sharing stories from her childhood, other times offering life advice wrapped in humor and tenderness. It wasn't just cooking; it was storytelling, connection, and love all rolled into one.

To this day, a pot of grits reminds me of her. It reminds me of home, of mornings spent around the table, of laughter and warmth shared over bowls of golden comfort. And even now, no matter how far life takes me, a bite of "Georgia Ice Cream" feels like coming home.

Reflections on Tradition

Grits carry a certain symbolism in the South—they're simple yet profound, a staple that speaks to the importance of grounding your-self in the essentials. They mirror life itself: a reminder that the best moments are often the simplest ones, seasoned with love and shared in good company.

Philosophically, grits evoke the idea of presence and community. Like the Southern tradition of slowing down and savoring the mo-ment, they remind us to linger—to appreciate what's in front of us and to honor the hands that made it. In the words of Wendell Berry, *"Eating is an agricultural act."* It connects us to the land, to the people who nourish us, and to the history we carry forward with every spoon-ful.

The Lesson of Nourishment

My mother's cheese grits were more than just food; they were a lesson in the art of nourishing not just the body, but the soul. They taught me the value of tradition, of cooking with love, and of taking the time to create something that brings joy to others. And in their own humble way, they remind me it's not about the grandeur—it's about the heart.

A Reader's Reflection

Let me offer a reflection:

- *Think of a dish that reminds you of home—one that carries memories of family, love, and tradition. What does it teach you about the connection between food, place, and the people who make it special?*

A Southern Story: The Front Porch Swing

There's something about a front porch swing that feels like the heartbeat of the South. It's a place where time slows, where the world seems to shrink to the size of your surroundings, and where countless conversations, confessions, and contemplations have found their home. Growing up, our swing was a well-worn fixture of the porch—its wood smoothed by years of hands gripping its frame, of feet nudging it into motion, of lives being lived and shared in its presence.

The porch swing was where my father would sit in the evening, a glass of sweet tea balanced precariously on the armrest, as he watched the sunset bleed colors into the sky. It's where my mother would hum old hymns, her hands busy shelling peas or mending a shirt. And it's where I'd find myself, often late at night, lost in thought under a canopy of stars, the rhythmic creak of the swing like a metronome for my wandering mind.

The swing wasn't just a piece of furniture—it was a place of stories. It heard the laughter of neighbors swapping tales, the sighs of someone who needed to unburden their heart, and the silence of a soul finding peace in the company of the night's stillness. It was a meeting place, a sanctuary, and a reminder that sometimes, the most meaningful moments happen when we allow ourselves to pause and simply be.

Reflections on the Porch Swing

The porch swing is a symbol of the Southern way of living—a life that values slowness, connection, and reflection. It's where we're reminded to linger, to savor the rhythm of life, and to embrace the company of others, even in the quietest of moments.

Philosophically, the swing represents balance and flow. It moves back and forth, steady and unhurried, teaching us that life, too, has its own natural rhythm. As Marcus Aurelius wrote in *Meditations*: *"Look well into thyself; there is a source of strength which will always spring up if thou wilt always look."* The swing invites us to do just that—to look inward, to reflect, and to find strength in the stillness.

The Lesson of the Swing

The front porch swing teaches us that life's richness isn't in constant motion but in the pauses—the moments when we let go of the rush, sit a spell, and open ourselves to the beauty of the present. It reminds us that the best stories, the deepest connections, and the most profound insights often come when we least expect them.

A Reader's Reflection

Here's a thought for you to reflect on:

- *Think of a "porch swing" in your life—a place where you find stillness, reflection, or connection. How can you create more time to linger there and embrace the lessons it offers?*

A Southern Story: The Sound of Sunday

There's a sacred stillness in the South on Sunday mornings, the kind that feels like the world is holding its breath. And then, breaking through the quiet, comes the sound of church bells—a melody that rises and falls, drifting across fields and over rooftops like a thread pulling the community together. It's not just a call to worship; it's a call to connect, to pause, and to belong.

As a child, those bells were my wake-up call. They'd start faint and distant, coaxing me out of sleep, and then grow louder, as if to say, *"It's time."* Time to lace up my shoes, don my Sunday best, and pile into the neighbor's car for the short drive to church. My mother always sat in the front seat, her hands folded in her lap, muted yet full of purpose, while my father remained at home working the fields.

The drive was its own ritual—past neighbors waving from their porches, past the oak trees that seemed to touch the sky, and past the small cemetery where generations of families rested. By the time we reached the church, the bells were at their fullest, echoing off the white clapboard siding and the stained-glass windows that caught the morning light.

Inside, the sanctuary was alive—a hum of whispered greetings, the shuffle of hymnals, the occasional burst of children's laughter. But for me, the bells always stood out. Even as the service began, their echo seemed to linger, a constant reminder of the world outside the church walls and the rhythm of life that continued on.

Reflections on the Bells

The church bells represent more than just a call to gather—they're a symbol of constancy in a changing world. Their sound is a thread through time, tying together past, present, and future, reminding us that faith, community, and tradition endure even as life shifts around us.

Philosophically, the bells resonate with the idea of shared experience. Their sound doesn't belong to one person; it belongs to everyone within earshot, uniting people in a single moment. It's a reminder of what Thomas Merton wrote: *"The deepest level of communication is not communication, but communion."* The bells create a communion—a moment where differences fade and what remains is the simple, powerful act of being together.

The Lesson of the Bells

The church bells teach us to listen, not just with our ears, but with our hearts. They remind moments of gathering, reflection, and stillness punctuate us, and that in those moments, we find a connection to something greater than ourselves.

A Reader's Reflection

Let me ask you a question:

- *Think of a sound that carries meaning in your life—a sound that reminds you of family, faith, or community. What does that sound teach you about connection and constancy?*

A Southern Story: The County Fair

When summer rolls in, bringing heat thick enough to make the pavement shimmer, there's one Southern tradition that promises a break from the monotony—a county fair. It's a place where the air smells of popcorn and cotton candy, where laughter echoes through the chaos of games and carnival rides, and where every corner seems to hum with the buzz of possibility.

I remember one fair in particular, back when I was still wide-eyed and full of wonder. The lights of the Ferris wheel glimmered like stars fallen to earth, casting their glow over the crowds below. There were booths lined with jars of preserves, prize-winning pies, and quilts so intricate they looked like they carried stories stitched into every thread. And then, of course, there was the livestock barn—a bustling hub where kids proudly paraded their prized pigs and cows, their faces glowing with a mix of pride and nerves.

For me, the fair wasn't just an event—it was an adventure. It was the thrill of flipping rings onto milk bottles, the dizzying spin of the Tilt-A-Whirl, and the satisfying crunch of a fresh funnel cake dusted with powdered sugar. It was the laughter of strangers, the reunion with old friends, and the steady rhythm of a small-town band playing under the stars. The fair was messy, loud, and gloriously alive—a celebration of all the quirks and charms that make the South feel like home.

As Ralph Waldo Emerson once said, *"Life is a festival only to the wise."* The county fair embodies this wisdom, reminding us that life's richness is found in moments of joy, connection, and celebration.

Reflections on the Fair

The county fair is more than just fun and games; it's a microcosm of Southern life—where tradition meets community, and where people come together to share in the joys of the moment. It's a reminder that even amidst the noise and chaos, there's beauty to be found in connection, celebration, and the shared experience of simply being present.

Philosophically, the fair mirrors the idea of abundance—not just in the sense of prizes and treats, but in the richness of life itself. It's a celebration of what we have and what we share, teaching us to embrace the moments that bring us together.

The Lesson of Celebration

The county fair teaches us to find joy in the ordinary—the smell of fried food, the laughter of a friend, the simple pleasure of wandering through a crowd. It reminds us that life's best moments don't have to be big or perfect; they just have to be shared.

A Reader's Reflection

Let me invite you to reflect on your own experiences through this prompt:

- *Think of a tradition or event that brings your community together, like a fair or festival. What makes it special to you, and how does it reflect the values and connections of the people around you?*

A Southern Story: The Crossroads at the Old Oak

Down the end of a gravel road, past fields that seem to stretch forever, there's a spot where two dirt paths meet under the shade of an old oak tree. It's the kind of place you might pass without much thought, but for me, it's always felt like a marker—both in the landscape and in life. People made choices here, paths diverged here, and countless journeys started here.

The first time I stood at those crossroads, I was just a boy, my bare toes curling into the dust as I tried to decide which path to take. To the left was a trail that wound through the woods, filled with the promise of adventure and discovery. To the right, the road stretched back toward the comforts of home, familiar and safe. I didn't know it then, but that moment mirrored countless decisions I'd face later in life—moments when I'd have to choose between the unknown and the familiar, between risk and comfort, between staying put and pressing on.

Years later, I returned to that crossroads, this time as an adult with the weight of life's decisions resting on my shoulders. I stood under the same oak tree, now gnarled with age but still steadfast, and felt the pull of memory and meaning in that place. The paths looked the same, but I knew that the choices they represented had grown infinitely more complex. And yet, as I stood there, I realized the lesson of the crossroads: it's not just about which path you take—it's about the way you walk it, with courage, intention, and faith in the journey ahead.

Reflections on the Crossroads

The Southern landscape is full of crossroads like this, both literal and metaphorical. They remind us that life is a series of choices, each one shaping the road ahead in ways we may not immediately see. As Ralph Waldo Emerson once said, *"Do not go where the path may lead, go instead where there is no path and leave a trail."* Crossroads challenge us to carve our own way, to embrace the unknown, and to trust in the path we choose.

Philosophically, the crossroads reflects the tension between fate and free will—a theme explored by thinkers from Aristotle to Camus. They remind us that while we may not control every circumstance, we always have the power to decide how we respond, which path we walk, and how we carry ourselves along the way.

The Lesson of the Crossroads

Standing at a crossroads is rarely easy, but it's in those moments of decision that we grow. The old oak at the meeting of paths teaches us that roots matter, but so does the courage to step forward, even when the road is uncertain. It's not about avoiding mistakes—it's about finding meaning in the journey.

A Reader's Reflection

Let's connect your own feelings about crossroads with this prompt:

- *Think of a "crossroads" moment in your life—a time when you had to choose between two paths. How did you decide, and what did the journey teach you about yourself and the world around you?*

A Southern Story: The Crossroads in Nashville

At fifteen, I stood at a crossroads—not just a figurative one, but a literal one, right there at the Greyhound bus station with a round-trip ticket to Nashville in one hand and a guitar case slung over my shoulder. It wasn't just a bus ticket; it was my passage to a dream. In my heart, I was already a country music star, ready to make my mark on Music City. All I needed was someone to take a chance on me—to hear the songs I'd poured my soul into and see the potential that burned bright in my childish heart.

Hope filled the ride to Nashville; the kind that makes the world feel wide open. I carried a small suitcase packed with just the essentials, along with the weight of expectation—mine, my family's, my friends'. Staying at the YMCA because it was cheap, I spent every daylight hour walking up and down 16th Avenue, the beating heart of the country music industry. With every step, I imagined my songs finding a home, my name lighting up marquees, and my voice joining the ranks of legends.

But dreams, I would soon learn, don't always unfold the way you hope. Rejection became the name of the game. At every door I knocked on, people politely but steadfastly refused, if not, showed outright indifference. No one took a chance on my songs, and the hope I'd carried felt heavier with every "no." By the end of the week, my pride was bruised, my suitcase a little lighter, and my guitar case still filled with unsung dreams.

It was with a heavy heart that I used my return ticket, making my way back to the Greyhound station. The journey home was quieter, the excitement replaced by a mix of disappointment and determination. Facing my family and friends wasn't easy. I felt the sting of rejection and the weight of unspoken questions: *What happens now? Where do I go from here?*

Reflections on the Crossroads

The crossroads in Nashville taught me a lesson I've carried ever since—that pursuing your dreams takes courage, and that courage doesn't diminish in the face of rejection; it grows. As Henry David Thoreau once said, *"Go confidently in the direction of your dreams. Live the life you have imagined."* Even if the journey doesn't lead where you expected, the act of trying, of showing up for your dreams, is its own kind of success.

Philosophically, the Nashville chapter reflects the importance of resilience. It's about understanding that rejection isn't the end of the road—it's a bend in it, a chance to reevaluate, to grow, and to press on. It's a reminder that the courage to try sets us apart, and that even unfulfilled dreams leave us richer for the attempt.

The Lesson of Persistence

Standing at a crossroads with a suitcase and a guitar case in hand, I learned that the path of dreams is rarely smooth, but it's worth walking. It's the act of trying, of daring to step forward into the unknown, that shapes us. And even when the world says "no," there's something deeply valuable in saying "yes" to yourself.

A Reader's Reflection

Let me offer you a thought to ponder:

- *Think of a moment when you stood at your own crossroads, chasing a dream or taking a risk. What did you learn from that journey, and how has it shaped the road you're walking now?*

The Crossroads at Sunset

The air was heavy that evening, thick with the scent of honeysuckle and the faint tang of the swamp just beyond the hill. The sun, a low-hanging ball of fire, lingered on the horizon, throwing long shadows across the dirt roads that met under the old pecan tree. Tommy Johnson stood there, his guitar case slung over his shoulder, as if the weight of it was all that tethered him to the earth. His eyes, dark and thoughtful, scanned the horizon, where the roads stretched out like lifelines—one leading toward the glow of town lights, the other disappearing into the wild unknown.

In the South, the crossroads was never just a place; it was a stage, a place where stories were born and destinies decided. Folks would talk about the deals made there, whispering tales of men who gambled their souls for a shot at greatness. Tommy's name would be one of those whispered, though whether his story was legend or truth depended on who was telling it.

They'd say Tommy knelt right there in the dust, his guitar in his lap, his fingers brushing the strings like he was praying. He'd made his plea to the devil, not in fear but in determination—a boy from the Delta who knew what he wanted and was willing to give up everything to get it. And when he rose, brushing the dirt from his knees, they'd say his guitar sang like it had never sung before, the notes so sweet and haunting they carried all the pain and beauty of the South in their sound.

Reflections on the Crossroads

The crossroads represents more than just the meeting of paths; it's a place of transformation, where choices are made that shape not just lives, but legacies. Like Atticus Finch's steadfast morality or Scout's coming-of-age wisdom, Tommy's story reminds us of the quiet strength required to face life's intersections with clarity and resolve.

There's a Southern elegance to the way these tales unfold, a cadence that captures both the weight of decision and the beauty of risk. As Robert Frost once wrote, *"Two roads diverged in a wood, and I—I took the one less traveled by, and that has made all the difference."* For Tommy, the road he chose defined him, not just as a musician, but as a symbol of the South's resilience, creativity, and deep connection to the land and its stories.

The Lesson of the Crossroads

Tommy's story teaches us about the courage it takes to chase our dreams, even when the stakes are high. It reminds us that the paths we choose aren't just about where they lead—they're about how we walk them, the music we make along the way, and the legacy we leave behind.

A Reader's Reflection

Here's a question to reflect on:

- *Think of a crossroads you've faced—a moment where the choices felt monumental. How did you navigate the intersection, and what song has your journey written since?*

A Southern Story: The Crossroads of Kindness

There was a spot in town where three roads met—a dusty intersection flanked by a gas station, an old general store, and a diner whose sign had faded over the years to an almost unrecognizable shade of blue. It wasn't much to look at, just another Southern crossroads in a town that didn't make the map, but to those who lived nearby, it was something more. It was a place where lives brushed up against each other—sometimes for a fleeting moment, sometimes forever.

I remember one summer evening, sticky with the kind of heat that makes the air shimmer, standing at that crossroads with a flat bicycle tire and no pump to fix it. I was just a kid then, fidgeting nervously in the shadow of the general store, not sure whether to head home or hope for help. That's when old Mr. Elmore walked out of the diner, carrying a Styrofoam cup filled with iced tea and a knowing smile.

"Looks like you got yourself stuck," he said, his drawl as slow and steady as the creak of his rocking chair back home. Without waiting for a reply, he knelt down beside the bike, inspecting the tire with the practiced ease of someone who'd seen a problem or two in his day. Moments later, with the tire patched and the bike as good as new, he leaned back, wiping his hands on the towel slung over his shoulder.

"Now," he said, his smile widening, "you be sure to pass it on next time someone's stuck."

It wasn't a dramatic gesture, not the kind that makes headlines or sticks in history books. But to me, standing there at that intersection, it felt monumental. The kindness of a stranger at a simple Southern crossroads taught me more about life's connections than any classroom ever could.

Reflections on the Crossroads

This story reminds me of the subtle power of kindness—the way small acts ripple outward, carrying with them a message of hope and humanity. As Maya Angelou once wrote, *"People will forget what you said, people will forget what you did, but people will never forget how you made them feel."* Mr. Elmore's kindness at the crossroads wasn't just about fixing a tire; it was about making someone feel seen, valued, and supported.

Philosophically, the crossroads represents the meeting of lives—the brief intersections where paths align and stories intertwine. It's a reminder that life's most meaningful moments often happen when we slow down enough to notice someone else's journey.

The Lesson of Kindness

At that Southern crossroads, I learned that the smallest gestures can leave the deepest marks. Mr. Elmore's act of kindness taught me that we're all connected, and that every intersection is an opportunity to make someone else's road a little smoother.

A Reader's Reflection

Let me invite you to connect with this tale with a thought to ponder:

- *Think of when someone's kindness helped you through a cross-roads in your life. How did it shape your journey, and how can you pass that kindness on to someone else?*

A Southern Story: Passing Yourself

There's an old Southern saying, wise in its simplicity, that my mother used to tell me: *"You run so fast that one day you're gonna pass your-*

self!" She'd say it with that gentle but knowing tone that only mothers seem to master—a tone that carried both humor and a warning. Back then, I'd laugh it off, too busy chasing life to pause and hear the deeper message. But as the years have gone on, her words have taken on a resonance I can't ignore.

In the South, life has a rhythm—a pace defined by the steady creak of a porch swing, the hum of cicadas in the summer heat, the slow brewing of sweet tea. It's a rhythm that teaches us to linger, to savor, to be present. Yet, for so many of us, there's a temptation to outrun it—to fill every hour with movement, every moment with action, every thought with ambition. And in doing so, we risk forgetting why we're running in the first place.

My mother's wisdom echoes an even older one from the Psalms: *"Be still, and know that I am God."* This timeless truth calls us to pause—not just physically, but spiritually. It's an invitation to step back from the race, to quiet the noise, and to reconnect with the source of all peace and purpose. In the stillness, we rediscover not just God, but ourselves.

Reflections on Speed and Stillness

My mother's saying reminds me of a deeper truth, one echoed by poets, philosophers, and scripture alike: that life isn't about how fast you can get from one moment to the next. It's about the richness of the journey—the stillness, the reflection, the connection. As the poet Mary Oliver famously asked, *"Tell me, what is it you plan to do with your one wild and precious life?"* Her words remind us, as my mother's and the psalmist's do, that life's meaning is found in the moments when we stop running long enough to see what's around us.

This saying also carries a subtle warning: that speed can turn into chaos, and chaos into exhaustion. When we run too fast, we risk passing ourselves—becoming disconnected from our own values, our own purpose, and the people who matter most. It's a reminder that balance matters—that the race isn't worth winning if we lose ourselves along the way.

The Lesson of Slowing Down

In the South, slowing down isn't just a choice; it's a way of life. It's in the deliberate act of shelling peas on the porch, of watching the fireflies dance at dusk, of taking the time to truly listen when someone says, "How're you doing?" My mother's saying—and the scripture she unwittingly mirrored—taught me that when we slow down, we don't just avoid passing ourselves, we find ourselves.

A Reader's Reflection

By reflecting on this wisdom, let's pose this thought:

- *Think of a time when life felt like it was moving too fast. What did you miss in the rush, and how can you create space to slow down, be still, and reconnect with the things that matter most?*

A Southern Story: A Song in the Storm

The South knows storms like an old friend—unpredictable, fierce, and always commanding attention. I remember those summer evenings when the horizon would darken, the air would grow thick with tension, and the first rumble of thunder would creep in from the distance. Mama had a way of knowing when a storm wasn't just passing through; she could feel it in her bones, as if the wind whispered its intentions just to her.

When the storms came, Mama never panicked. Instead, she'd gather us children, her voice calm but firm. "Come on, now," she'd say, ushering us under the old homestead, a house held aloft on brick pillars that seemed to creak in protest with every gust of wind. Beneath the house, the earth was cool and damp, smelling faintly of soil and the occasional lost toy we'd forgotten to retrieve. Mama would huddle us close, her arms like a fortress, her presence steady as the storm raged above.

And then she'd sing. Oh, how Mama would sing. Her voice, clear and unwavering, would rise above the roar of the wind and the sharp cracks of thunder. She'd choose hymns—old, familiar ones like *"It Is Well with My Soul"* or *"Amazing Grace"*—songs that carried not just melody but meaning, their words, a shield against the fear that threatened to seep into our small hearts. One night, the storm was unlike anything we'd ever seen. The sky turned a sickly shade of gray, the wind howled like a wild animal, and the rain fell in torrents so thick it seemed to blur the world beyond. Mama held us tighter that night, her voice stronger than ever, as if daring the storm to outdo her. And then it came—the unmistakable roar of a tornado, its ferocity so near we could feel the vibrations in the ground.

The house shuddered, the air felt electric, and for a moment, it seemed like the world might break apart. But through it all, there was Mama's voice. Singing, unwavering, defiant. Her hymns cut through the chaos, a reminder that no storm, no matter how fierce, could silence the strength of a mother's love and faith.

When the storm passed, leaving a path of broken trees and scattered debris, Mama finally stopped singing. She looked each of us in the eyes, her face calm and steady, and said, "See? We made it through." And we had—not just through the storm, but through the fear, held firm by her voice and her presence.

Reflections on the Storm

This story isn't just about weathering a storm; it's about the power of resilience and faith in the face of chaos. Mama's singing was more than just a distraction—it was a declaration. It was her way of saying that no matter how dark the sky, there is always light to be found in the strength of love and the comfort of belief.

As Psalm 32:7 reminds us, *"You are my hiding place; you will protect me from trouble and surround me with songs of deliverance."* Mama's hymns were those songs of deliverance, carrying us through the storm and teaching us that courage doesn't mean the absence of fear—it means standing firm amid it.

The Lesson of the Storm

The storms of life, like the weather, are inevitable. But what matters most is how we face them. Mama's singing taught us that even in the darkest moments, we have the power to bring light—to find strength, to offer comfort, and to hold on to faith that the storm will pass.

A Reader's Reflection

Let me offer you a moment of reflection:

- *Think of a storm you've faced—literal or metaphorical. What gave you strength in that moment, and how can you carry that strength forward into the storms yet to come?*

A Southern Story: The Heart of the Fruit Stand

Just down the dirt lane from our house, where the gravel met the highway and the air smelled faintly of peaches and wildflowers, stood the seasonal fruit stand. It wasn't much to look at—a simple wooden structure with a tin roof that creaked in the wind—but it was the pulse of our little community, beating steadily through the warm months of the year.

From April through September, the fruit stand came alive with the colors of the South: the fiery orange of Florida citrus, the blush-pink of Georgia peaches, the golden glow of jars filled with honey harvested just down the road. It was a place where the seasons revealed themselves, not through a calendar but through the sweet smell of ripening pears or the first arrival of muscadines in August. For us, it wasn't just a convenience; it was a ritual, a rhythm, a reminder of the bounty that surrounded us.

But looking back, the fruit stand offered more than just fruits and vegetables. It offered connection. It was a gathering place, where neighbors stopped to exchange recipes, news, and kindnesses alongside their produce. Farmers and artisans alike shared the fruits of their labor at this place—literal and figurative—celebrating the land that sustained us. And it was a bridge, connecting the old ways with the new, the rural with the bustling highway that carried travelers to places we could only imagine.

Reflections Beyond the Fruit

The fruit stand teaches us something profound about life—that nourishment isn't just about what feeds the body, but what feeds the soul. It's about community, about the connections that grow when people come together to share the fruits of their labor and their lives. In a world that often moves too fast, the fruit stand represents the importance of pausing, of savoring, of recognizing the beauty in life's small but meaningful exchanges.

Philosophically, it mirrors the idea of abundance—not just in the sense of produce, but in the richness of shared experience. As Wendell Berry writes, *"The earth is what we all have in common."* The fruit stand was a microcosm of that truth—a place where the land's bounty became a shared blessing, weaving people together in a tapestry of interdependence and gratitude.

The Lesson of the Fruit Stand

The fruit stand reminds us that life's greatest treasures are often found in the simplest of places. It teaches us to honor the work of the hands that till the soil, to value the relationships that grow in the shade of a summer afternoon, and to see every exchange—not just of goods, but of words, smiles, and stories—as an opportunity to connect. It challenges us to live with intention, finding nourishment not just in what we consume, but in how we engage with the world.

A Reader's Reflection

Let me invite you to reflect on your own experiences with places of connection and community.

- *Think of a place in your own life that represents more than what it offers on the surface—a market, a park, or even a front porch. What does it teach you about connection, community, and the value of pausing to savor life's abundance?*

A Southern Story: Writing the Pages of Life

Life, my friend, is so much more than just the number of pages in a book. It isn't about how thick the volume is, how many chapters it holds, or how quickly it's read. No, life is about what's written on those pages—the words, the stories, the emotions that leap off the paper and into the hearts of those who turn them. It's what fills the spaces between the lines that makes all the difference.

Each day, we write a new page. Some are ordinary—a grocery list scrawled hurriedly in the margins, a brief exchange with a neighbor, the quiet satisfaction of making it through. Others are extraordinary—bold, italicized moments of love, adventure, heartbreak, and triumph. But together, they create the narrative of a life, a story uniquely ours. And the beauty of it is, no two books are the same.

My mother, ever the poet without knowing it, used to say, *"Every morning is an empty page, and it's up to you to fill it."* She'd challenge me to write the kind of story worth telling, to make the words count. Her wisdom taught me it wasn't about rushing to the end of the book or worrying about how long the story would be. It was about savoring the process, crafting each chapter with care, and filling every page with intention.

Reflections on a Life Well-Written

My philosophy on life, hopefully, reminds you that a meaningful life isn't measured in years, but in moments. It's not about how many pages we live, but how vividly we live them. As poet Ralph Waldo Emerson once wrote, *"Write it on your heart that every day is the best day in the year."* Every page is an opportunity—a blank slate waiting for the ink of our experiences, our choices, our connections.

Philosophically, this idea mirrors the concept of living deliberately, as Thoreau might put it. It's about focusing not on the quantity of life's moments, but on their quality—on writing a story that's true to who we are and reflective of the impact we hope to leave on others. A book with a few meaningful pages can have far more power than one filled with empty words.

The Lesson of the Pages

My philosophy, if it's worth anything, teaches us that life's richness lies not in its length, but in its depth. It invites us to slow down, to be deliberate about the story we're telling, and to ensure that each page carries the weight of our values, our dreams, and the love we share with those around us. It challenges us to ask: *What story am I writing today, and how will it live on in the hearts of others?*

A Reader's Reflection

Let's turn this reflection outward and invite others to engage.

- *Think of the story you're writing with your life. What do you want the pages to say about you, and how can you fill today's page with meaning, love, and purpose?*

A Southern Story: The Two Seasons of the South

In the South, we like to keep things simple. Up North, they speak of four seasons—each with its own charm, its own personality. But down here, we know better. We've only got two seasons, and they're as distinct as sweet tea and unsweet tea: summer and winter.

Summer, or what others might call spring, stretches out with a vengeance. Summer arrives bold and unapologetic the moment the last frost melts into the earth. The days grow long; the sun blazes high, and the air wraps around you like a damp, suffocating hug. There's no mistaking its presence—mosquitoes swarm, garden tomatoes ripen faster than you can eat them, and iced tea glasses sweat as much as the people holding them. It's the season of porch swings creaking late into the evening, of county fairs and cicadas, of firecrackers lighting up humid July nights.

Then there's winter—a season that's less a grand entrance and more a reluctant nod to the calendar. It doesn't linger long, mind you, and it's not what others would call truly cold. But when it comes, we grab our jackets (or just a good sweater) and pretend it's frigid while the temperature hovers somewhere above freezing. Winter is the season of pecan pies, family reunions, and smoky wood fires curling up into the clear night sky. It's a fleeting, welcome pause from the relentless heat, a reminder to gather close before the cycle begins again.

Reflections on the Two Seasons

Life in the South is shaped by this rhythmic dance between extremes—summer's endless sprawl and winter's brief interlude. It teaches us to adapt, to lean into the heat when it comes, and to cherish the cool moments while they last. There's wisdom in the way Southerners live by the seasons, unhurried and attuned to the land's rhythms. As Thoreau once said, *"Live in each season as it passes; breathe the air, drink the drink, taste the fruit."*

The two seasons also serve as metaphors for life itself—moments of abundance and activity, followed by periods of rest and reflection. They remind us that life is cyclical, that each season carries its own beauty and lessons, and that there's value in embracing both the heat and the chill.

The Lesson of the Seasons

The seasons of the South teach us that balance is key. Summers test our patience and endurance, while winters remind us to pause, reflect, and reconnect. Together, they create a rhythm that keeps life vibrant, challenging, and deeply rooted in the present moment.

A Reader's Reflection

Here is a question to reflect on:

- *What are the seasons of your own life—moments of heat and intensity, and times of rest and reflection? How can you embrace the lessons that each season offers?*

A Southern Story: The Road to Redemption

The road into town was a long stretch of asphalt lined with fields that seemed to touch the sky, broken only by the occasional barn or weathered fence post. It was a road I had traveled a thousand times, but one summer evening, it felt different—heavier, quieter, as though the earth itself knew what I carried with me.

I'd done something I regretted, something that left a fracture in my small world. Nothing earth-shattering in the grand scheme of things, but enough to leave me standing at a crossroads, wondering if I'd ever be able to make it right. Mama always said, *"Grace isn't earned—it's given. But that doesn't mean you shouldn't go looking for it."* And so, I walked this old familiar road, searching for something I couldn't quite name.

The path led me to Mr. Henry's front porch. He was the kind of man whose silence said more than most folks' words, and who could somehow tell what was on your heart before you ever spoke it. As I climbed the steps, he was already there in his rocking chair, a glass of iced tea in his hand and a calm, steady look in his eye.

"Evenin'," he said, his voice low and slow, like honey dripping from a spoon. I nodded, unable to find the words to begin. He didn't press, just motioned to the empty chair beside him. And so we sat, the crickets filling the silence with their chorus, the sun sinking low over the fields. Finally, I found the courage to speak, stumbling through the weight of my mistake, the regret that had been eating at me, and the question that hung in the air: could I ever make it right?

Mr. Henry listened, his gaze fixed on the horizon, until I fell silent. Then he leaned forward, placing his glass carefully on the porch rail. *"Ain't nobody walks this earth without a misstep or two,"* he said. *"The question ain't whether you can make it right. The question is what you'll do with the lesson once you've learned it."*

His words sat heavy and sweet, like the scent of the jasmine growing along the porch. Redemption, I realized, wasn't about erasing the mistake—it was about what came next. It was about showing up, facing the people I'd hurt, and proving, little by little, that I could be better.

Reflections on Redemption

The road to redemption isn't a straight path—it's winding, messy, and often humbling. It's a journey that requires both courage and grace, not just from those seeking it, but from those willing to offer it. As the writer Anne Lamott says, *"Grace means you're in a different universe from where you had been stuck, when you had absolutely no way to get there on your own."* Mr. Henry's wisdom reminds us that redemption isn't about perfection; it's about progress, about finding the strength to stand back up after a fall and walk forward with intention.

The Lesson of Grace

In the South, grace is as much a part of life as the sweet tea and porch swings. It's in the way we forgive, the way we rebuild, and the way we choose love over judgment. The road to redemption teaches us that mistakes are inevitable, but they don't define us—what matters is what we do afterward, how we grow, and how we extend the same grace we hope to receive.

A Reader's Reflection

Let me leave you with something to reflect on:

- *Consider a time when you received a second chance, or when you offered one to someone else. How did that moment shape your understanding of grace, and what did it teach you about the power of redemption?*

A Southern Story: The Night Watchman

Down the dirt lane from my childhood home, past the whispering pines and the occasional glow of fireflies, stood the Turpentine still. The surrounding air was always rich with the scent of pine, a sticky sweetness that seemed to linger in the back of your throat. It was a place of mystery and allure, its lights cutting through the night like beacons. And it was there that I found an unlikely friend and mentor—the Night Watchman.

Most kids my age wouldn't have given the old Turpentine still a second thought, but to me, it was a world waiting to be discovered. I'd sneak down the lane after supper, when the sky turned from blue to inky black, to join the Watchman on his nightly rounds. Armed with his clocking key and the steady beam of his flashlight, he'd make his way from one checkpoint to the next, and I'd follow along, my small footsteps falling in time with his.

The Night Watchman wasn't a man of many words, but when he spoke, his voice carried the weight that made you stop and listen. He'd talk about life, about the way the world worked, and about the lessons he'd learned from walking his path. I soaked it all in, like a sapling soaking up sunlight, eager to grow in his shadow.

"Charles," he said one night, as we clocked in at the far end of the property, *"life ain't always as sticky as this pine tar. There's always a way out of your troubles. You just got to keep your nose to the grindstone."* I remember looking up at him, the light from his flashlight casting long shadows across his face and feeling the truth of his words settle into my young mind like the still's tar settling into barrels.

Reflections on the Night Watchman's Wisdom

The Night Watchman taught me more than just how to clock in or navigate the still in the dark—he taught me the value of persistence, of finding strength even when life feels sticky and tangled. His words were simple but profound, a reminder that no matter how tough things get, there's always a way forward if you're willing to put in the work.

His philosophy mirrors the wisdom of the South itself—a land that knows the power of resilience, of grit, of pushing through the hard times with faith that better days are ahead. It's a lesson that holds true whether you're walking the rounds at a still, sitting on a porch with sweet tea in hand, or facing one of life's countless challenges.

The Lesson of the Night Watchman

The Watchman's guidance reminds us that life's stickiest situations don't have to hold us back—they can teach us to find solutions, to persevere, and to grow. It's not about avoiding the pine tar; it's about learning how to clean your hands and keep moving forward. And most of all, it's about finding mentors along the way who help light your path and teach you the lessons you need to carry onward.

A Reader's Reflection

I invite you to connect with this story by reflecting on your own mentors.

- *Think of someone who offered you wisdom at a pivotal moment in your life. What did they teach you, and how has their guidance shaped the way you face life's challenges?*

A Southern Story: Playing for Mister Mac

In our little town, Mister Mac was more than just the city supervisor—he was a legend, though he'd never claim it himself. Blind in one eye, with a pitch that could send us scrambling out of the batter's box, he might not have been the most precise coach, but to us, he was the best there ever was.

He took us country boys, raw and eager, and turned us into champions—not just on the scoreboard, but in spirit. His practices were a mix of chaos and encouragement, his voice booming across the diamond like a freight train. *"Keep your eye on the ball!"* he'd shout, though we all knew it wasn't the ball we were watching—it was him.

Mister Mac wasn't the kind of coach who barked or belittled. He was a cheerleader in a baseball cap, lifting us up with his unwavering belief in our potential. And oh, how we wanted to prove him right. We played our hearts out for him, running harder, swinging truer, and diving farther, not just for the wins, but for the grin that would light up his face when we succeeded.

Off the field, Mister Mac's impact was even greater. His office door was always open, a sanctuary for any of us who needed to talk, to laugh, or just to sit in the quiet comfort of his presence. He didn't preach or pry; he listened, and in his steady way, he taught us that life was about more than the game. It was about showing up for each other, about working hard and staying true, about finding joy in the small victories.

I'll never forget the day he handed me my first pair of baseball shoes, or the weight of the catcher's mitt he gave me—the first one I'd ever owned. They weren't just gifts; they were symbols of his belief in me, in all of us. He gave us more than equipment; he gave us confidence, and in doing so, he gave us a piece of himself.

Reflections on Mister Mac

Mister Mac's story is a reminder that mentors don't have to be perfect to be extraordinary. His pitches might've kept us on our toes, but his heart never wavered—it was steady, generous, and full of love for the boys who played under his guidance. He taught us that a true coach isn't measured by wins or trophies, but by the lives they shape and the lessons they leave behind.

As baseball legend Joe DiMaggio once said, *"A person always doing his or her best becomes a natural leader, just by example."* Mister Mac didn't have to try to lead—he did it effortlessly, through his actions, his encouragement, and his unwavering belief in the power of a team.

The Lesson of Mister Mac

From Mister Mac, we learned that life, like baseball, is about more than just the plays. It's about showing up, putting your heart into every moment, and cheering for others along the way. He reminded us that even when the odds aren't in your favor—whether you're blind in one eye or facing a stronger team—faith, effort, and camaraderie can carry you farther than you ever imagined.

A Reader's Reflection

Let me invite you to reflect on the impact of your own mentors with this question:

- *Think of someone who believed in you, who cheered you on even when you didn't believe in yourself. What did they teach you, and how can you carry their legacy forward in your own life?*

A Southern Story: My First Taste of Love

It was a warm evening, the kind where the air seemed to hum with possibility, as Mama and I made our way thirty miles down the highway to a house tucked deep in the Georgia countryside. The occasion was a pickin' and singin' night, a gathering of folks who brought their instruments, their voices, and their stories to share. For me, it was a chance to learn, to soak up the music, and maybe even strum along with the band. But I had no idea that the night would hold something far more unforgettable.

The house was alive with sound—guitars strumming, voices harmonizing, and the steady rhythm of feet tapping on the wooden floor. I had just started learning to play guitar, and my fingers itched to join in. But before I could even open my case, I saw her. She was standing near the porch, her black hair swept up in a bouffant that seemed to defy gravity, her smile as bright as the lanterns strung across the yard. She was beautiful in a way that made my thirteen-year-old heart skip a beat.

She caught my eye, and before I knew it, we were talking, her voice as sweet as the melodies drifting from the house. *"Wanna go for a walk?"* she asked, and I nodded, my words caught somewhere between my throat and my chest. We slipped away from the music, the laughter, and the clinking of mason jars, stepping onto the dirt road that stretched out into the quiet night.

We walked slowly, the gravel crunching beneath our feet, until we reached a fence row that seemed to glow in the moonlight. There, we stopped and talked—about everything and nothing, about dreams and music and the kind of things that only seem important when you're young and the world feels wide open. Her laughter was soft, her presence magnetic, and for that hour, it felt like time had paused just for us.

And then it happened. She leaned over the fence, her eyes sparkling, and kissed me. It was my first kiss, and it sent my head spinning, my heart racing, and my world tilting on its axis. In that moment, I was certain she was the love of my life, the girl I'd been waiting for without even knowing it.

But as all moments do, it ended. Her father's voice called us back to the house, and we returned to the music and the crowd, our secret tucked away like a treasure. I never saw her again, but for years, I dreamed of her sweet face, her laughter, and that kiss by the fence row. It was a memory that stayed with me, not as a regret, but as a reminder of the beauty of first love—the kind that's pure, fleeting, and unforgettable.

Reflections on First Love

First love is a rite of passage, a moment that stays with us long after it's passed. It's not just about the person or the kiss—it's about the way it makes us feel alive, hopeful, and connected to something bigger than ourselves. As poet, Lord Byron once wrote, *"In her first passion, a woman loves her lover, in all the others, all she loves is love."*

The Lesson of First Love

First love teaches us that life is made up of moments—some fleeting, some lasting, but all meaningful. It reminds us to embrace the present, to cherish the connections we make, and to carry the sweetness of those memories with us as we grow. It's a lesson in vulnerability, in joy, and in the beauty of simply being human.

A Reader's Reflection

Let me invite you to reflect on your own first loves with this question:

- *Think back to your first taste of love. What did it teach you about yourself, about connection, and about the way love shapes our lives?*

A Southern Story: The Bull That Wasn't

It was one of those pitch-black nights when the moon seemed to have taken leave, leaving the world cloaked in shadows. For three boys with mischief on their minds, it was the perfect setting for an adventure—or so we thought.

My two friends and I had hatched a plan, fueled by the kind of daring that only comes with youth and a lack of foresight. We were headed to Mr. Farmer's livestock field, a place where cows dotted the pasture by day like lazy clouds but, at night, became perfect targets for some harmless pranks. The idea was simple: scare the cows, watch them scatter, and laugh until our sides hurt. What could possibly go wrong?

We crept down the country road, the gravel crunching softly under our feet, until we reached the fence line. The field stretched out before us, a sea of shadows and faint outlines. With barely a whispered warning, we climbed over the fence, our hearts pounding with the thrill of mischief.

But then we heard it—a low, rumbling sound, followed by the unmistakable rustle of movement. In the dark, a hulking silhouette emerged, its mass unmistakably larger and more menacing than any cow we'd ever seen. A bull. Or so we thought.

Before we could even think, the figure started toward us, its pace quickening as it closed the distance. Panic took over. We turned tail and ran as fast as we could, tripping over lumpy soil, shoes flying, and arms flailing. When we couldn't run any farther, we dropped to the ground, curled into balls, and covered our heads, bracing for the worst.

The moments that followed felt like an eternity. My heart hammered in my chest, every second stretching out like a lifetime. And then it happened—something warm and wet brushed against my hand. A tongue. I dared to peek through my fingers, and there she was: Bell, Mr. Farmer's trusty Labrador retriever, her tail wagging like this was the greatest game she'd ever played.

The realization hit us all at once, and what had been fear dissolved into uncontrollable laughter. Bell barked playfully, oblivious to the terror she'd just caused, and we clambered to our feet, shaking with relief and glee. What we had mistaken for a raging bull had been nothing more than an enthusiastic dog looking to join the fun.

We never returned to that field again, but the memory of that night stayed with us, a reminder of the humor that can be found in our most foolish moments. For days, we laughed until our sides ached, retelling the story and embellishing it with every round. Bell became a legend in her own right—the dog who scared the mischief out of three boys on a moonless night.

Reflections on Misadventures

Stories like this remind us of the innocence and sheer unpredictability of youth. They teach us to laugh at ourselves, to find joy in the ridiculous, and to appreciate the small moments that make life so delightfully unpredictable. As Mark Twain once said, *"Humor is mankind's greatest blessing,"* and nights like that are proof of it.

The Lesson of Bell

What started as a mischievous plan turned into a lesson in humility, humor, and the kindness of a dog who could turn fear into laughter with a single lick. Bell taught us that sometimes, the scariest moments in life are the ones we'll laugh about the hardest later on.

A Reader's Reflection

Let me invite you into the spirit of this tale with a reflection:

- *Think back to a misadventure that left you laughing for days. What did it teach you about fear, humor, and the unexpected twists that make life memorable?*

A Southern Story: From Rock to Redemption

The summer evenings in our small Southern town had a way of stretching out, the fading light of day lingering like a whispered promise. It was the place where people's names carried stories, where conversations unfolded slow as molasses and where faith was the thread that bound the patches of the community quilt. That was the setting for the day Donnie came to school and changed everything.

Donnie wasn't just a drummer; he was the heartbeat of our little rock band, the steady rhythm behind every chord, every lyric. But on this day, he seemed different, quieter somehow, his usual cheer tempered by something deeper. I'd known him long enough to see when something was weighing on his heart, and as he took his seat beside me, I braced myself for whatever news he carried.

"You know, Charles," he began, his voice low but unwavering, *"something happened to me last night. I—I gave my life to God."* The words hung in the air between us, heavy and full of meaning. As he went on, explaining the conviction he'd felt, the peace he'd found, and his decision to stop playing rock music, I felt a mix of emotions I couldn't untangle—devastation for what it meant for our band, and a quiet, unspoken hope that maybe, just maybe, he'd found something I hadn't even realized I was searching for.

With Donnie's departure, the band faded into memory, but he wasn't done with me yet. *"Come with me to this meeting,"* he said one day, his tone insistent but kind. *"Campus Crusade for Christ. Just try it."* And so, one evening, I sat in a room surrounded by strangers, the sound of music and prayer filling the air like the cicadas that hummed in the Georgia night.

At first, I felt out of place, like a guest at a dinner table where I didn't know the hosts. But as the night went on, something shifted. It wasn't dramatic—not the kind of moment you'd write about in headlines. It was muted, subtle, like the first breeze after a sweltering day. My heart, restless as the tide, felt strangely warmed. And when the time came, I stepped forward, not out of fear or obligation, but out of something I couldn't quite name—a yearning to surrender, to belong, to believe.

That night was the beginning of a journey that would stretch across fifty-three years. The rock songs I once played gave way to gospel melodies, songs that carried the message of hope and grace I'd found in that small, unassuming room. With time, the music became more than an expression; it became a calling. I wrote and recorded seventeen albums of original songs, each one a reflection of the faith that had taken root in my heart.

But the music was only the first step. As the years passed, I felt another pull—the call to ministry, to walk alongside others as they found their own warmth, their own surrender, their own purpose. It wasn't always easy, but it was always worth it. And now, as I stand at the threshold of retirement, I don't see an ending; I see a legacy, a life shaped by grace, and a friend's courage to share his truth.

Reflections on Transformation

In the South, transformation often begins quietly, like the turning of a season or the blooming of wildflowers after the frost. It's a place where faith is both personal and communal, where redemption is a story told not in chapters but in lives. My journey mirrors that Southern rhythm—steady, meaningful, and deeply rooted in the soil of grace.

Like Atticus Finch's unwavering morality or Scout's journey to understanding, hopefully my story reminds us that life's greatest lessons often come not in grand gestures, but in small, honest moments of change. It's about finding courage in vulnerability, strength in surrender, and purpose in love.

The Lesson of Redemption

This tale teaches us that redemption isn't just about letting go; it's about embracing what comes next. It's a reminder that life's music doesn't end when the melody changes—it simply shifts to a tune more profound, more beautiful, and more lasting.

A Reader's Reflection

Let me invite you to connect with this story:

- *Think back* to when *you felt called to make a change. How did it transform your journey, and what legacy are you leaving behind as a result?*

A Southern Story: The Gift of Mercy

The Southern sun has a way of shining a little too brightly on certain days, almost as if it's trying to unearth the secrets we'd rather keep buried. I remember such a day, one that began with a laugh among friends and ended with the cold clang of steel bars behind me. I was just a boy then, full of mischief and foolish courage, skipping school with two pals who had hatched a plan that now makes my heart heavy just to recall. We would break into a few homes, they said—quick, easy, and daring. What could go wrong?

Everything, as it turned out. Before the sun had even begun to set, we found ourselves caught, the city police officer standing over us with an expression that mixed weariness and disappointment. It wasn't long before we were sitting in the county jail, the weight of our choices pressing down like the thick Georgia humidity. Two and a half months passed in that place, the days creeping by, each one heavier than the last. And when the time came, the verdict was clear: one year in a Georgia detention center.

But then something remarkable happened. The judge, a man whose stern countenance belied the kindness stirring in his heart, had a change of mind—or perhaps, a change of heart. It was the day before

Christmas when he called us to stand before him again, his voice firm but laced with mercy. *"Go home,"* he said. *"Spend Christmas with your families."*

It felt like grace, pure and undeserved, falling like snowflakes on a Southern Christmas Eve. I returned home that day a different boy, humbled by the weight of what could have been and overwhelmed by the mercy that had spared me.

That act of grace became a seed, planted deep within my soul. Over time, it grew into a calling—a desire to give back, to guide others, to help those standing at the same crossroads where I once stood. I became a community worker with Juvenile Court Services, walking alongside kids whose lives mirrored my own wild youth. I saw myself in their eyes, their restlessness, their struggles, and I made it my mission to show them the same kindness that had been shown to me.

But the story didn't end there. That mercy became a thread, leading me into a life of ministry—a life dedicated to serving the God who had spared me when I deserved it least. For fifty-three years, I walked this path, carrying the lessons of that Christmas Eve with me: that mercy is not something we earn, but something we are given, and that in receiving it, we are called to share it.

Reflections on Mercy and Redemption

My story speaks to the power of a second chance—a reminder that even in our darkest moments, there is light waiting to guide us back to the path we're meant to walk. It's a testament to the transformative power of grace, both human and divine, and to the incredible things that can happen when we let that grace shape our lives.

As Southern wisdom often reminds us, *"There, but for* the grace *of God, go I."* My journey shows how true that is, how mercy can not only change a life but inspire a lifetime of service, compassion, and purpose.

The Lesson of Grace

Hopefully, my story teaches us that our past does not define us—our choices in its wake do. It reminds us that mercy is not just a gift to be received, but a responsibility to be shared. And it shows us that even the most unlikely paths can lead to lives of profound meaning and impact.

A Reader's Reflection

I invite you to reflect on your own experiences of mercy.

- *Think of a time when you received a second chance. How did it shape the person you've become, and how can you extend that same grace to someone else?*

Let's Bring this Home to Roost:

The South has a way of leaving its fingerprints on a life, shaping it with its rhythm and grace, its storms and songs. It's a land of first loves and mischief, of wisdom passed from mentors like heirlooms, and of mercy so sweet it feels like spring rain on a parched field. My stories are rooted in that soil, and together they tell of a boy becoming a man, a seeker finding purpose, and a heart learning to give what it once received.

We wandered through tender memories of a moonlit kiss, the kind that lingers like the scent of honeysuckle on a July night. We laughed at a wide-eyed boy's misstep when Bell, the trusty Labrador, turned terror into laughter under a moonless sky. And we listened closely to the lessons of steadfast mentors—the Night Watchman, Mister Mac, and a kind judge—who offered wisdom as steady as a front porch swing, shaping not just my choices but my character.

My path hasn't been a straight one—it's wound through shadowed woods, over lumpy soil, and into the sunlit fields of redemption. From the mercy that spared me to the music that called me, these stories speak to the resilience of a soul shaped by both its scars and its blessings. They tell of a man who faced the crossroads, who found the courage to step forward, and who turned his life into a song worth sharing.

And now, as we draw this chapter to a close, it's not an ending—it's a resting place, a pause to take in the view and savor the journey before stepping onto the next road. For a Southern soul knows that life isn't bound by chapters; it's a series of seasons, each one a gift, each one a chance to grow deeper, wider, and truer.

3

The Philosophy of a Southern Life

L ife down here has a rhythm all its own, slower than the rush of
the world beyond, but steady as the heart of an old grandfather
clock. It's a place where truth is spoken not in fancy words but in
the muted wisdom of a neighbor's nod or the flicker of fireflies on a
summer night. Philosophy here doesn't come from books stacked high
on dusty library shelves—it rises from the soil, whispers in the breeze,
and stretches out in the shade of pecan trees.

The South has a way of teaching you things without ever seeming
to try. It's in the smell of rain on red clay, in the creak of porch swings,
and in the way the sun keeps its vigil over endless rows of cotton. Life is
simple here, but never shallow. The mornings take their time coming
up over the hills, and the nights linger just long enough to remind you
that stillness is as important as motion.

Reflection: *What lessons am I missing in the rush of my own days?*
Could I slow down enough to hear the truths hiding in silence?

But life in the South is also about resilience. This land knows what
it means to face storms—the kind that flood the creeks and the kind
that shakes the soul. And yet, it keeps growing, keeps blooming, keeps
reaching for the sky. It's a place where hope and faith hold their
ground, where a farmer tends his fields with hands worn from years

of labor, trusting that the seeds he's sown will find the strength to rise.

Reflection: *When have I found resilience within myself, and what did it teach me about the strength I didn't know I had?*

And then there's connection. Here, life isn't lived alone—it's shared, passed from hand to hand like a well-loved recipe for biscuits or cobbler. Whether it's a potluck on a Sunday afternoon or a church choir harmonizing beneath stained-glass windows, the South teaches you that joy multiplies when it's shared and burdens shrink when carried together.

Reflection: *Who are the people who've shaped me, and how can I honor the gift of their presence in my life?*

Finally, the South is a place that invites reflection. It nudges you to sit for a spell, to look out over the fields, and to let the past speak. The creak of a rocking chair is an echo of stories once told, and the long shadows of the day remind you that life, like the land, shifts and changes but always holds its roots.

Reflection: *What values have guided my path, and how can I live a life that reflects the truths I hold close?*

Philosophy here isn't fancy or complicated—it's as simple and profound as the call of a whippoorwill at dusk. It's about asking the questions that matter, about listening for answers in the places we least expect and about finding meaning not in grand gestures but in the muted, everyday rhythms of life. And it's about remembering that sometimes, the greatest truths come not from what we say—but from what we pause long enough to hear.

The Rhythm of Time and Memory

In the South, time feels different—as though the days stretch wider and the seasons linger longer, giving you space to breathe, to think, to remember. Time is both kind and relentless here, moving forward without pause but leaving its fingerprints in every corner of your life. It whispers to you through creaking floorboards, through the soft lines etched into the faces of old friends, through the warmth of sunlight filtering through kitchen curtains unchanged by years gone by.

Memory, too, carries its own rhythm—surfacing when you least expect it, tethering you to moments you thought you'd forgotten. The South teaches us to honor our memories, not as a burden, but as a gift. They are like wildflowers growing along a dirt road, unexpected and fleeting, but beautiful if you pause long enough to look.

Reflection: *What memories have shaped you, and how do they guide your present journey? How can you hold on to the rhythm of time without rushing to* outrun *it?*

Faith and Perseverance

If the South teaches resilience, it also teaches faith—the kind that binds you to something greater than yourself, whether it's God, nature, or the steady rhythm of community. Faith here isn't just a belief; it's a practice, lived out in kindness to neighbors, in prayers spoken over fields, and in unwavering hope when all seems lost.

Perseverance walks hand-in-hand with faith, reminding us that no storm lasts forever and that every step forward, no matter how small, is an act of courage. Think of the farmer who rebuilds after the floodwaters rise or the mother who stays steady through sleepless nights of worry.

Reflection: *When have you leaned on faith to carry you through hard times, and how has it strengthened your resolve to keep moving forward?*

Nature as Teacher

The South is full of teachers, but none are as constant or wise as the land itself. The fields, the rivers, the skies—they carry lessons that reveal themselves slowly, like seeds growing into trees. Nature teaches us patience, reminding us that good things take time, whether it's a harvest, a healing, or a dream. It shows us the importance of balance, the interplay between growth and rest, between roots and wings.

And perhaps most importantly, nature teaches us gratitude. Its rhythms, its beauty, its muted strength—they remind us to cherish the world, to see it as a gift.

Reflection: *What has nature taught you about yourself? How can its lessons guide your own rhythms and choices?*

The Philosophy of a Southern Morning

Morning comes softly here, with sunlight filtering through lace curtains and the smell of coffee brewing on the stove. For some, it's a time of ease, of rising slowly to greet the day. But for others, mornings bring their own kind of reckoning—a reminder of the aches, the pills, the surgeries that mark the passage of years. It's the South's way of nudging you to face life head-on, even when the burdens feel heavier than you'd like to carry.

Seventy-four years is a long stretch of road, but the South knows how to remind you that each mile counts. Every creak of a knee, every pill swallowed, every scar from surgeries past—they're proof of a life lived, of a body that's weathered storms and kept going.

Reflection: *What marks have my journey left on me, and how can I embrace them as symbols of strength rather than signs of decline?*

But age in the South isn't about giving up—it's about pushing on, about believing that the best is still ahead even when the shadows of doubt creep in. It's about looking at the obituaries, seeing names and faces you recognize, and reminding yourself that today you woke up, you breathed, you lived. It's about knowing that every morning is a gift, no matter how heavy the body feels. And it's about holding onto the hope that life still has beauty waiting for you in the moments yet to come.

This philosophy isn't something you find in sermons or books; it's in the way the South calls you to keep showing up, to keep fighting, to keep dreaming. It's the same resilience that holds up a barn after decades of storms or keeps flowers blooming along fence rows when the soil feels too tired to give.

Reflection: *What keeps me going each day, even when it's hard? How can I find joy in the act of perseverance?*

And in the end, it's faith that steadies the spirit when the body grows weary—faith that each ache and scar tells a story worth hearing, faith that life's meaning isn't diminished by its struggles, and faith that there's peace waiting beyond that final breath. It's a faith as Southern as magnolias in bloom, rooted deep and weathered strong.

Lessons for the Reader

- *See the marks of time as badges of honor—not proof of weakness, but proof of resilience.*

- *Remember that every day you wake up is another chance to live with purpose, to find joy in the small things, and to keep moving forward.*

- *Hold on to hope, even when the road feels steep, and trust that life still has beauty waiting just around the bend.*

Morning's Reckoning

Charles E. Cravey

The dawn breaks soft, its golden glow.
Through lace-trimmed curtains, it starts to show,
A body weary, scars to wear,
A tale of time etched here and there.

Six pills to keep the rhythm right,
Five more swallowed as falls the night.
Bones that creak, a back long worn.
Yet every day, a new day born.

Seventy-four, "just seventy-four,"
I tell myself there's still much more,
Though names and faces fill the page,
I push ahead despite my age.

For life is not the aches it brings,
But all the hope beneath its wings,
And every breath, until it's gone,
A gift to cherish, to carry on.

So let the pills and pains be small,
For faith and joy outshine them all,
And when the dawn comes shining through,
It whispers softly: *There's more for you.*

Reflection on Grace in Challenges

Life tests us in ways that seem insurmountable, yet these trials often become the proving grounds for our character. As Friedrich Nietzsche once said, *"That which does not kill us makes us stronger."* The South teaches us to see every challenge not as an end, but as a beginning—an opportunity to grow in resilience and grace.

Reflection: *How have my struggles shaped me, and what strength have they revealed within me?*

Reflection on Gratitude for Time

Time in the South feels different—patient, deliberate, and deeply rooted in the rhythm of life. As Marcus Aurelius observed, *"You could leave life right now. Let that determine what you do and say and think."* Time is a gift, reminding us to savor each fleeting moment.

Reflection: *Am I living with intention, or letting time slip away unnoticed? How can I embrace the beauty of this moment, even amidst life's challenges?*

Reflection on Endurance Through Faith

Faith steadies us when the road ahead seems unclear, offering hope when life feels heavy. Søren Kierkegaard reminds us that *"Faith sees best in the dark."* It's in the muted trust that grace will carry us through, even when we cannot see the way forward.

Reflection: *When have I leaned on faith to guide me, and how has it helped me endure life's storms?*

Reflection on Hope in Aging

Growing older is not a loss but a gift—a chance to see life's tapestry from a wider vantage point. As Ralph Waldo Emerson reflected, *"The years teach much which the days never knew."* Age invites us to celebrate wisdom gained through time, to find joy in the journey rather than lament its passage.

Reflection: *How can I honor the richness of my years and embrace the beauty of growing older?*

Reflection on Embracing Imperfection

Life isn't perfect, nor is it meant to be. The South reminds us that flaws are where the light gets in, where authenticity and truth reside. As Leonard Cohen poetically remarked, *"There is a crack in everything. That's how the light gets in."*

Reflection: *What imperfections in my life can I learn to see as blessings rather than faults? How can I turn my flaws into strengths?*

Quotes that Anchor the Reader

Let's offer a few additional quotes to echo the spirit of Southern philosophy:

- *"Happiness depends upon ourselves."* — Aristotle

- *"Do not dwell in the past, do not dream of the future, concentrate the mind on the present moment."* — Buddha

- *"Man is not made for defeat."* — Ernest Hemingway

- *"The unexamined life is not worth living."* — Socrates

Reflection on the Balance Between Loss and Gratitude

Life has a way of teaching us that gain and loss are two sides of the

same coin. For every moment of joy, there's a shadow of imperma-
nence; for every loss, there's a gift hidden in its wake. The South, with
its muted resilience, reminds us to carry both gratitude and grief in our
hearts, like two harmonizing melodies. As Kahlil Gibran wrote, *"The
deeper that sorrow carves into your being, the more joy you can contain."*

Think of the fields after a storm—though battered, they remain
fertile, ready to bloom again when the rains pass, and the sun returns.

Reflection: *What losses have shaped me, and how can I hold grati-
tude for what remains? How can I honor what I've lost while celebrating
what I've received?*

Reflection on the Quietness of Wisdom

Wisdom doesn't always speak loudly; sometimes, it comes in whis-
pers—a word from a friend, the rustle of leaves in the wind, or the
stillness of a morning dew-covered field. The South knows the value of
silence, of pausing long enough to hear the truths that escape a hurried
life. As Lao Tzu famously said, *"Silence is a source of great strength."*

The stillness of a southern afternoon teaches us to find beauty in
muted places, to let our minds rest and our hearts listen.

Reflection: *How can I seek wisdom in silence? What truths have I
overlooked because I was too busy to hear them?*

Reflection on the Courage of Authenticity

In the South, there's no room for pretense—life demands that you
show up as you are, with all your flaws and all your grace. It teaches us
the courage of authenticity, the strength of being real in a world that
often rewards facades. As Oscar Wilde observed, *"Be yourself; everyone
else is already taken."*

Authenticity isn't about perfection; it's about honesty, about letting the cracks in our armor reveal the light within.

Reflection: *How can I embrace my true self and let go of the need to appear flawless? How can I live in a way that reflects my deepest values and beliefs?*

Reflection on the Unfinished Symphony of Life

Life is a song that's always in progress—an unfinished symphony made beautiful by its imperfections. The South understands this deeply; it's in the way a porch swing creaks in the wind, or a handwritten letter leaves room for smudges. As Leonardo da Vinci once said, *"Art is never finished, only abandoned."*

To live is to accept that not everything will be resolved, not every note will be perfect, but the beauty lies in the effort, the love, the trying.

Reflection: *What unfinished parts of my life can I embrace as works in progress? How can I find joy in the journey rather than waiting for a perfect conclusion?*

Reflection on the Threads That Bind Us

No one exists in isolation; our lives are woven together like the threads of a quilt, each one unique but part of a greater whole. The South thrives on connection, on relationships that feel like lifelines in times of trouble and anchors in the winds of change. Aristotle aptly said, *"Man is by nature a social animal."*

The shared potluck, the Sunday service, the neighborly wave across a dirt road—these remind us that life gains meaning through the people we share it with.

Reflection: *Who are the threads in my tapestry, and how can I strengthen those bonds? How can I show gratitude for the connections that* *have shaped me?*

A Southern Call to Reflection

These reflections invite you not to rush past the moments that define life but to pause, consider, and carry forward the wisdom gleaned from muted mornings, long roads, and the hum of cicadas at dusk. As we expand this chapter, the aim is to create a rich narrative of meaning that resonates deeply, not just with the intellect, but with the heart.

The Philosophy of Legacy: The Cross That Tells a Story

Legacy isn't written in stone or etched in grand monuments; it's passed on in the quiet, enduring things that hold meaning beyond the years. In the South, legacy often finds its roots in the simple and the sacred—an old quilt passed through generations, a handwritten recipe folded into memory, or a wooden cross carved from the knee of a cypress tree.

For fifty years, I've carried my cross—a gift born not just of wood, but of the bond between friends and the craftsmanship of hands guided by thoughtfulness. Its grain, naturally forming the shape of a cross, is a story all its own etched by nature, finished by human care. On Sundays, while sermons echoed through sanctuary walls, that cross stood as silent testimony to my calling. It adorned my presence in life's most profound moments—marriages celebrated, lives remembered, hope rekindled.

Yet, a legacy's strength is not just in the things we treasure, but in the meaning we pass along with them. By entrusting this cross to my son, I'm weaving its story into a new chapter—one rooted in my ministry and devotion, but extending into his own journey. The grain of the wood will hold his hand as it once held mine, carrying with it the faith, love, and endurance I've built over a lifetime.

As Marcus Aurelius reminds us, *"What we do now echoes in eternity."* Legacy isn't just about leaving something behind; it's about inspiring others to carry it forward with pride, purpose, and their own story to tell.

Reflection: *What treasures in my life hold meaning beyond their surface? How can I ensure the values and love behind them endure in the lives of those who come after me?*

Legacy in the Fabric of Life

The story of my cross reminds us that legacy is rarely about grandeur; it's about the quiet impact of a life well-lived. Like the grain in the wood, legacy grows naturally from the choices we make, the kindness we offer, and the love we share. It's not about perfection but about authenticity—a reminder that even the simplest things can carry the deepest meaning.

For readers, this story is an invitation to consider their own legacies. What objects, traditions, or lessons are they passing down? How can they ensure that the stories behind them—the faith, the resilience, the humanity—are just as enduring as the items themselves?

A Reader's Reflection

I invite you to ponder these questions:

- *What piece of your life would you pass on to someone you love, and what story would it tell about you?*

- *How do your daily choices shape the legacy you'll leave behind?*

- *What simple things in your life hold meaning beyond their surface, waiting to be shared with others?*

The Philosophy of Forgiveness: The Strength to Let Go

Forgiveness isn't just an act—it's a journey, one that starts in the heart and stretches out to touch everything around it. In the South, forgiveness often comes wrapped in the muted resilience of people who understand what it means to make mistakes, to be hurt, and to seek peace. It's found in the wisdom of elders who remind us that holding onto anger is like carrying a heavy sack of stones—it only weighs us down and keeps us from walking forward.

Mahatma Gandhi once said, *"The weak can never forgive. Forgiveness is the attribute of the strong."* And he was right. Forgiving someone, or even yourself, requires courage—courage to face the hurt, to let go of resentment, and to believe in the possibility of change. It's not about excusing wrongs or forgetting pain; it's about releasing the hold they have on you and choosing grace over bitterness.

Forgiveness in the South often takes root in the soil of faith, grounded in the belief that grace is given to us so that we might extend it to others. It's in the preacher who welcomes back a lost soul, the neighbor who lends a helping hand despite old disputes, the family member who says, *"I understand,"* when words fail.

Reflection: *When have I been hurt, and how* can forgiveness *free me from carrying that pain? How can forgiving someone else also bring healing to my own heart?*

But forgiveness doesn't always come easily—it's a process, one that requires patience, humility, and a willingness to let go of pride. It's the quiet act of saying, *"I release you,"* even when the apology never comes, even when the hurt still lingers. As Nelson Mandela observed,

"Resentment is like drinking poison and then hoping it will kill your enemies." Forgiveness is not just for them; it's for us, for the freedom it brings, for the peace it restores.

The Gift of Self-Forgiveness

In the South, where storytelling reigns, there's a saying that echoes across generations: *"You're only human."* It's a simple reminder that we all stumble, we all fall, and we all need to forgive ourselves for the mistakes we've made. Self-forgiveness is often the hardest kind of grace to give, but it's the most necessary. It's the act of looking in the mirror and saying, *"I did wrong, but I can do better,"* and then taking steps toward that better.

Ask yourself: *What mistakes do I need to release? How can I be kinder to myself and embrace the growth that comes from imperfection?*

Lessons in Forgiveness

Let's reflect on these questions:

- *Who in your life have you struggled to forgive, and what would it take to release that burden?*

- *What hurts are you holding on to, and how might forgiveness set you free?*

- *How can forgiving yourself allow you to live with greater peace and purpose?*

The Philosophy of Storytelling: Truth Wrapped in Tales

In the South, stories are currency—they're traded over porch rails and dinner tables, in barbershops and church pews. To tell a story here is to share a piece of your soul, to offer not just entertainment but connection, wisdom, and understanding. A good story isn't just heard—it's felt, carried in the heart like a favorite hymn.

The act of storytelling is as old as humanity itself, stretching back to nights when our ancestors gathered around fires to share the triumph of a hunt or the lessons learned in hardship. As Joan Didion wrote, *"We tell ourselves stories in order to live."* Storytelling gives shape to chaos; it takes the threads of our experiences, our joys, and struggles, and weaves them into something meaningful.

In the South, every story has its own rhythm, its own heartbeat. There's the slow drawl of a tale told under a sprawling oak tree, the lively cadence of a joke shared at a fish fry, the quiet intimacy of a memory whispered in the stillness of night. These stories connect us—not just to each other, but to the past, to the land, to the values that guide our lives.

Reflection: *What stories have shaped me? What wisdom or humor do I carry forward in the tales I tell?*

The Power of Stories to Heal

Stories don't just entertain; they heal. A well-told story can mend a broken heart, offer solace to a weary soul, or light a path through darkness. As Brené Brown said, *"Maybe stories are just data with a soul."* When we tell our stories, we're not just sharing facts—we're sharing truths, fears, hopes, and dreams that resonate far beyond the teller's voice.

Consider the grieving parent who finds comfort in the stories told at a wake, or the struggling teenager who discovers strength in the pages of a novel. Storytelling reminds us we're never truly alone, that someone, somewhere, has walked a similar path and found their way through.

Reflection: *What stories in my life have brought me comfort, and how can I share my own to lift others up?*

Lessons in Storytelling

A good story doesn't have to be grand—it just has to be honest. The South teaches us that the best stories are the simple ones, the ones that come from the heart and reflect the truth of who we are. Consider these questions:

- *What story do I want to leave behind for others to tell?*

- *How can I use storytelling as a way to connect with others, to share wisdom, and to bring light into the world?*

- *What truths do my own stories reveal, and how can I share them authentically?*

Storytelling as the Heartbeat of Community

In the South, storytelling is the glue that holds communities together. Whether it's tales shared around a church potluck, gossip whispered over a backyard fence, or family histories recounted by the glow of a fire, stories connect us in ways that words alone cannot. They remind us that we belong to something larger—that our lives are intertwined, like threads in a quilt stitched by loving hands.

Community storytelling carries lessons, humor, and wisdom. It teaches us to laugh at ourselves, to see the humanity in others, and to find strength in knowing we're not alone. As Margaret Atwood said, *"A word after a word after a word is power."* In this context, storytelling isn't just about entertainment; it's about empowerment—giving voices to experiences and turning memory into meaning.

Storytelling as a Bridge to Understanding

Stories have a way of breaking down barriers, of fostering empathy in a world that often struggles to see beyond its own borders. When you tell your story, you invite others to step into your shoes, to walk the paths you've walked, and to see the world through your eyes. It's an act of generosity, of saying, *"Here's who I am, and here's what I've learned. Maybe you'll find pieces of yourself in it."*

Consider Harper Lee's words from *To Kill a Mockingbird*: *"You never really understand a person until you consider things from his point of view...until you climb inside of his skin and walk around in it."* Storytelling does just that—it invites readers and listeners to climb inside your story and emerge with greater understanding.

Storytelling as a Keeper of Truth

The best stories carry truth in their heart, even when the details have grown fuzzy with time. The South reveres this kind of storytelling—the sort that offers wisdom in parables, which turns personal tales into universal lessons. Truth doesn't always need to be literal to be profound; it can shine through the moral of the story; the love poured into its telling.

Reflection: *What truths do my stories reveal? How can I share them in ways that inspire others to carry those truths forward?*

A Reader's Reflection

With these questions, perhaps you can share your own story.

- *What story from your own life carries the greatest meaning, and how can you share it with those you love?*

- *What stories have you inherited from others, and how can you preserve their wisdom for future generations?*

- *How can storytelling help you foster connection, understanding, and healing in your community?*

The Philosophy of Solitude and Reflection: Quiet Roads to Understanding

The South knows the value of solitude—not as loneliness, but as a chance to find ourselves in the quiet spaces of the world. A long walk down a dirt road, the stillness of a sunrise, the gentle lull of water flowing over stones—all of these offer moments to pause, to breathe, to reflect. Solitude is the act of stepping back from the noise of life, not to escape, but to listen. As Marcus Aurelius wrote, *"Nowhere can man find a quieter or more untroubled retreat than in his own soul."*

Reflection, like solitude, asks us to slow down enough to see what we've overlooked. It's not a luxury; it's a necessity—an act of self-care that helps us grow, understand, and move forward. Think of the farmer sitting by the creek after a long day's work, his mind drifting to seasons past and seasons yet to come. Or the teacher sitting in a rocker on a cool evening, letting the twilight guide her thoughts to lessons taught and lessons learned.

Reflection: *Where can I find solitude in my life, and how can I use it to grow deeper in understanding?*

Solitude as a Mirror for the Soul

In the South, solitude often finds its home in nature—in the stillness of the woods, the expanse of fields, the gentle sway of Spanish moss hanging from branches. Nature becomes a mirror, reflecting the truths we carry within ourselves, whether they're hopes, fears, or dreams. As Henry David Thoreau observed, *"I went to the woods because I wished to live deliberately, to front only the essential facts of life."*

The woods, the water, the land—they invite us to ask questions that matter. *Who am I when the world fades away? What do I truly value? What paths lie ahead, waiting for me to tread them?*

Reflection as a Path to Wisdom

Reflection isn't about looking back—it's about holding life's moments up to the light and seeing their patterns, their truths, their beauty. The South teaches us to honor the past without being bound by it, to let its lessons guide us toward a richer, fuller future. Reflection turns mistakes into wisdom, joys into gratitude, and losses into resilience.

Reflection: *What moments in my life deserve deeper reflection? What lessons have I missed because I haven't slowed down to find them?*

A Reader's Reflection

Let me invite you into your own journey of solitude and reflection:

- *Where can I find quiet moments in my life to pause and reflect on who I am and where I'm going?*

- *What truths have I overlooked because I haven't taken the time to listen to my heart?*

- *How can solitude help me reconnect with the values and dreams that guide my life?*

The Philosophy of Nature as a Teacher: Lessons in the Land

The South is a place of muted majesty, where the land itself becomes a teacher, whispering wisdom to all who stop long enough to hear. The hills, the rivers, the sprawling fields—they speak of patience, of resilience, of beauty found in the simplest things. Nature doesn't use words to teach its lessons; it uses the turning of seasons, the sway of branches, the silence before the storm. As Ralph Waldo Emerson beautifully said, *"Nature always wears the colors of the spirit."*

In the South, the land teaches patience. It reminds us that good things take time, whether it's the ripening of peaches in the summer sun or the slow growth of cypress trees rooted deep in swamp waters. We learn from the farmer who waits for the harvest, trusting that seeds will rise when the time is right.

Reflection: *What in* my life *requires patience, and how can I trust the process of growth?*

Nature also teaches resilience. Consider the river that wears down stone, not with brute force, but with steady persistence. Or the magnolia tree that blooms boldly even after a harsh winter. The land reminds us that strength isn't always loud—it's often quiet, deliberate, and rooted.

Reflection: *What storms in my life have I weathered, and how have they shaped the person I've become?*

And perhaps most importantly, nature teaches gratitude. Its beauty is everywhere, waiting to be noticed—the streaks of pink in an evening sky, the gentle hum of crickets in the dark, the scent of pine carried on the wind. It asks us to pause, to breathe, to see the world as a gift.

Reflection: *What small joys in nature have I overlooked, and how can I carry gratitude for them into my daily life?*

Nature as a Mirror for the Soul

In the stillness of the South, nature often reflects the truths we carry within ourselves. The calmness of a lake might mirror our own peace; the fury of a storm might echo the unrest in our hearts. As Henry David Thoreau said, *"I went to the woods because I wished to live deliberately, to front only the essential facts of life."* Nature becomes a canvas, inviting us to see our own emotions and dreams painted across its landscapes.

Consider the dawn breaking over a field—it holds a promise that each day begins anew, a reminder that no matter what's come before, there's always another chance to start again.

Reflection: *What does the natural world reflect to me about my own hopes, fears, and dreams?*

A Reader's Reflection

Please draw wisdom from nature's muted teachings:

- *What lessons can I learn from the patience of growing things, the resilience of the land, and the beauty of the seasons?*

- *How can nature inspire me to live with greater intention and gratitude?*

- *What truths about myself are waiting to be revealed in the stillness of the natural world?*

The Philosophy of Mortality: Death Makes Life Possible

Down here in the South, we don't shy away from talking about the big things—the rhythm of life, the ticking of time, and the inevitability of that last breath we all must take. Mortality isn't just a shadow we try to outrun; it's the muted truth that lingers in every sunrise and every whisper of wind through the tall pines. And as someone once said, *"Death makes life possible."*

Mortality teaches us to see the world through sharper eyes, to notice the things we might otherwise miss. It's in the way the honeysuckle blooms for just a season, its scent lingering sweet and fleeting. It's in the long hours before the storm, when the air grows still, and you realize how precious calmness can be. Life, like the land, is impermanent—and it's that very impermanence that makes every moment worth holding close.

Reflection: *If life's beauty is in its fleeting nature, how can I learn to treasure it more fully?*

Lessons From the Land

The South understands mortality in a way that feels rooted in its soil. It sees it in the cycles of planting and harvest, in the leaves that fall only to make room for spring's renewal. Death doesn't mean the end here—it means transformation, it means legacy; it means love carried forward in new and beautiful ways.

Consider the farmer who plants a grove knowing he'll never see it reach its full height, trusting that his grandchildren will sit beneath its shade. Or the widow who tends her husband's garden long after he's gone, finding pieces of his soul in every bloom. Mortality, in its muted way, invites us to think about what we'll leave behind—not in wealth or fame, but in moments of love, wisdom, and care.

Living More Fully

To look mortality in the eye is not to despair, but to live more fully. It's the knowledge that life is finite that makes each sunrise worth waking for, each laugh worth sharing, each love worth cherishing. The

South teaches this in its stories—stories of loss, yes, but also stories of resilience, joy, and the enduring belief that life is a gift worth celebrating.

As Emily Dickinson so poetically wrote, *"Because I could not stop for Death, he kindly stopped for me."* There's grace in the acceptance of mortality, and even in the face of it, there's room for hope.

Reflection: *How can the awareness of mortality inspire me to embrace life's small wonders?*

A Reader's Reflection

I invite you to consider your own relationship with mortality:

- *How does the impermanence of life inspire me to live with greater purpose and intention?*

- *What legacies am I creating that will endure long after I'm gone?*

- *How can I honor both the beauty and the brevity of life in the choices I make each day?*

Threads in the Tapestry: The South's Quiet Wisdom

Down here in the South, the air itself feels connected, like every breeze carries a story. Every morning light draws neighbors closer. Every shadow beneath the pecan trees holds secrets that tie us together. Life here isn't lived in isolation; it's shared, it's woven, it's felt. The South teaches us that we are threads in a tapestry far greater than ourselves, each one essential to the strength and beauty of the whole.

Interconnection isn't just about proximity—it's about belonging. It's about knowing that the porch light you leave burning might be the beacon someone needs. It's about trusting that the laughter you share today will echo in hearts for years to come.

Reflection: *What connections in my own life have shaped me into the person I am today? How have my choices, my kindnesses, and my stories created ripples I may never see?*

The Legacy of Kindness

The South thrives on kindness—not the flashy kind that seeks recognition, but the quiet kind that feels as natural as breathing. Consider the neighbor who mows your grass when you're too tired to ask, or the shopkeeper who lets you "pay him next time" because he knows times are hard. These simple acts don't just stay with the giver and receiver—they ripple outward, inspiring more kindness, creating a legacy of care and connection.

Maya Angelou reminds us, *"People will forget what you said, people will forget what you did, but people will never forget how you made them feel."* Kindness isn't bound by time; it lasts long after the moment has passed, embedding itself in the hearts of those it touches.

Reflection: *Who has shown me quiet kindness in my life, and how can I honor their generosity? How can I pass that kindness on to others, creating ripples that endure?*

The Choices We Leave Behind

Every choice we make—no matter how small—leaves a mark. The South sees this truth clearly, recognizing that decisions aren't isolated; they're threads woven into the lives of others, tying us to family, community, and the world beyond. It's in the way we choose to care for the land, to teach a child, to preserve a story worth telling.

As Jane Goodall observed, *"You cannot get through a single day without having an impact on the world around you."* Here in the South, that impact often takes the form of simple acts of love—the farmer who hands out fresh peaches at church, the elder who spends hours sewing quilts for those in need, the friend who listens even when the words are hard to hear.

Reflection: *What choices am I making that ripple outward, and what impact are they leaving on the lives of others?*

Interconnection Through Stories

In the South, stories aren't just told; they're shared. They're gifts that remind us we're part of something larger—pieces of a greater whole. When you tell a story, you invite others into your world, offering them the chance to see through your eyes and feel through your heart. Storytelling becomes an act of connection, a bridge that ties souls together.

Consider the words of Harper Lee: *"You never really understand a person until you consider things from his point of view...until you climb into his skin and walk around in it."* Stories invite us to walk around in someone else's world, to feel the connections we might otherwise overlook.

Reflection: *What stories do I carry that connect me to others, and how can I use them to inspire understanding and empathy?*

A Reader's Reflection

Let me encourage you to explore your connections:

- *What threads in my life tie me to others, and how can I strengthen those bonds?*

- *What acts of kindness have shaped me, and how can I pass their legacy forward?*

- *What stories do I tell, and how do they connect me to the world around me?*

The Philosophy of Joy: Sweetness in the Small Things

In the South, joy is as much a part of life as the cicadas singing at twilight or the gentle creak of a porch swing on a summer evening. It doesn't take much to find it here—it's in the first sip of sweet tea on a hot afternoon, in the sound of children laughing as they chase fireflies, in the way the sun filters through the leaves of an old oak tree. Southern joy isn't loud or showy; it's humble, quiet, and deeply rooted in the ordinary.

Joy, as they say, is a choice—a way of seeing the world that transforms the simplest moments into treasures. As Helen Keller once said, *"Joy is aglow."* In every corner of life, there's something to be grateful for, some small sweetness to savor.

Reflection: *What small moments in my life bring me joy, and how can I carry that joy into each day?*

The Resilience of Joy

Joy isn't about avoiding life's hardships; it's about finding light even in the shadowed places. The South knows this well—it's seen storms tear through its fields and trials weigh heavy on its people, yet still, joy persists. It's in the hymn sung during Sunday service, the shared meal after a long day of work, the laughter that bubbles up in moments of rest.

As Viktor Frankl, who found meaning even in the darkest of circumstances, said, *"Everything can be taken from a man but one thing: the last of the human freedoms—to choose one's attitude in any given set of circumstances."* Joy, then, is an act of resilience, a refusal to let sorrow have the last word.

Reflection: *How can I find joy even amid life's challenges? What moments of light have helped me through the darkness?*

Joy as Connection

The South understands that joy is best when it's shared. It's in the way a potluck gathers a community around one long table, in the way music brings people to their feet and into each other's arms. Joy connects us, reminds us that we're not alone, and strengthens the bonds that hold us together.

Think of the neighbor who waves as you pass, the friend who brings you a bouquet of fresh-picked wildflowers, the family that gathers under one roof to swap stories and laughter. These are the moments that remind us life is richer when it's shared.

Reflection: *Who are the people who bring joy into my life, and how can I bring joy into theirs?*

A Reader's Reflection

Let me guide you to embrace joy in your life.

- *What small things bring me happiness, and how can I make space for more of them in my days?*

- *How can I choose joy even when life feels hard, and how has resilience shaped my own happiness?*

- *What can I do to share joy with others, strengthening the connections that give life meaning?*

The Philosophy of Celebration: Finding Life in the Moments

In the South, celebration isn't reserved for grand occasions or fancy invitations—it's found in the little victories, the shared stories, the meals that bring people together. It's a backyard barbecue on a Sunday afternoon, the clink of iced tea glasses beneath the shade of a pecan tree, the way an entire town gathers to cheer for a high school football team on a crisp autumn night. Down here, life is celebrated not despite its imperfections, but because of them.

Celebration, like joy, is a choice. It's an act of defiance in a world that often focuses on what's lacking instead of what's abundant. It's about looking at a plate of fried green tomatoes and savoring each bite, about raising your voice in a hymn even if it cracks on the high notes, about dancing barefoot in the yard because the fireflies won't be here forever.

Reflection: *What small moments in my life are worth celebrating, and how can I honor them more fully?*

Celebration as Connection

The South has a way of making celebration contagious. You see it in the smiles passed around a dinner table, the way hands clap in rhythm during a bluegrass song, the way strangers become friends at a festival booth selling homemade peach cobbler. Celebration binds us together, reminding us that life's joys are richer when shared.

Even in hard times, celebration can be found in the gathering of people who care for one another. It's the way a neighbor brings over a casserole after a loss or the way family members find laughter amidst old photo albums during a wake. As Maya Angelou said, *"I've learned that people will forget what you said, people will forget what you did, but people will never forget how you made them feel."*

Honoring the Everyday

True celebration doesn't need decorations or grandeur—it needs presence. It's in the way you cherish an ordinary sunrise, the taste of biscuits fresh from the oven, the sound of rain on a tin roof. These moments, so easy to overlook, are the heart of life's beauty. To celebrate them is to live fully, to find gratitude in simplicity.

Reflection: *How can I celebrate the beauty of the everyday? What moments in my life deserve recognition, not because they're extraordinary, but because they're mine?*

A Reader's Reflection

I invite you to embrace the act of celebration:

- *What small triumphs in my life can I celebrate today?*

- *How can I create moments of connection and joy with the people around me?*

- *What overlooked parts of my daily routine might hold reasons for gratitude and celebration?*

The Philosophy of Gratitude: A Heart Full of Thanks

In the South, gratitude feels like second nature—it's in the way folks nod and say "thank you" even for the smallest kindness, in the way communities come together to help one another without expecting recognition. Gratitude here isn't just a fleeting feeling; it's a way of life, a lens through which people view the world.

Gratitude teaches us to see abundance even where there seems to be scarcity. It's the joy of breaking into a loaf of fresh cornbread, knowing every crumb is a blessing. It's the deep breath you take under an open sky, marveling at how many shades of blue there can be. As Melody Beattie wisely said, *"Gratitude turns what we have into enough."*

Reflection: How can *I embrace gratitude for what I have rather than longing for what I don't?*

Gratitude as Resilience

Life isn't always easy, but gratitude has a way of strengthening the soul, of turning hardships into lessons and struggles into stepping-stones. Down here, folks say, *"Count your blessings,"* not because life is without sorrow, but because blessings remind us of the good still shining through. The South knows the beauty of finding gratitude even in adversity—of thanking the land for its harvest even after a rough season, of finding hope in the laughter of children despite tough times.

As Oprah Winfrey expressed, *"Be thankful for what you have; you'll end up having more."* Gratitude magnifies joy and eases pain, turning a broken heart into fertile ground for growth.

Reflection: *How has gratitude helped me weather storms, and what blessings have carried me through even the hardest of days?*

Gratitude as Connection

Gratitude isn't just about feeling thankful—it's about sharing it, spreading it, multiplying it. The South understands this well. When someone lends a helping hand, the thanks they receive are genuine, heartfelt, and often returned in kind. A casserole delivered after a surgery, a warm hug in times of loss, a call to say "I appreciate you"—each act of gratitude strengthens the ties that bind us.

Think of the ripples a simple "thank you" can create. A kind word leads to a smile, a smile leads to kindness shared with someone else, and suddenly gratitude has found its way into the hearts of many.

Reflection: *Who in my life deserves a thank you, and how can expressing gratitude deepen* our connection?

A Reader's Reflection

I invite you to explore your own gratitude journey.

- *What blessings in my life am I most thankful for, and how can I honor them more fully?*

- *How has gratitude helped me find strength and perspective during challenging times?*

- *How can I share my gratitude with others, creating ripples of kindness and connection?*

The Philosophy of Resilience: Weathering Life's Storms

The South knows storms well—not just the kind that tear through skies with thunder and wind, but the ones that shake the soul and leave lives changed forever. Resilience here is a way of life, a strength that rises in the wake of hardship and keeps reaching for the light. Like the roots of a live oak tree deep in the soil, resilience holds steady, bends with the wind, and stands firm when the storms have passed.

Resilience isn't just about surviving—it's about thriving, about finding ways to grow through adversity. It's the farmer who replants his crops after the flood, trusting that the land will heal. It's the mother who rebuilds her family's strength after loss, stitching love and hope back together with patient hands.

Reflection: *What storms have I weathered, and how has resilience* *carried me through to brighter days?*

Lessons from the Land

In the South, the land itself teaches resilience. Think of the way a field blooms again after drought, or the way wildflowers find cracks in pavement and refuse to be stopped. Nature carries muted lessons in perseverance, reminding us that strength isn't always loud—it's often found in the patient, steady act of rising again.

As Maya Angelou so beautifully said, *"I can be changed by what happens to me, but I refuse to be reduced by it."* Resilience doesn't mean avoiding hardship; it means using it as fuel to grow stronger.

Reflection: *What lessons have I learned from the challenges I've faced, and how can I carry that strength forward into the future?*

Resilience as Hope

Resilience and hope walk hand in hand, reminding us that even in the darkest moments, there's always a reason to keep moving forward. The South finds hope in the small things—in the way sunlight breaks through after rain, in the hymn sung after loss, in the kindness of neighbors who lend their strength when yours feels spent.

Hope doesn't promise a simple path; it promises the strength to keep walking it.

Reflection: *How does hope guide me through hard times, and how has resilience shaped my ability to endure life's challenges?*

A Reader's Reflection

Let me encourage you to embrace your own resilience.

- *What moments in my life required strength I didn't know I had, and what did I learn from them?*

- *How can the lessons of resilience help me face challenges with greater courage and hope?*

- *What examples of resilience—whether in nature or in others—can inspire me to keep moving forward?*

The Philosophy of Hope: A Light That Never Fades

Hope is a Southern virtue—it's found in the songs sung beneath stained-glass windows, in the hands clasped in prayer, in the farmer who plants seeds knowing the harvest is uncertain. Down here, hope isn't loud or flashy; it's steady, unwavering, like the glow of fireflies on a warm evening. It's the belief that no matter how long the night feels, morning will come, bringing light with it.

Hope doesn't promise an easy road, but it promises the strength to walk it. It's in the way the river keeps flowing even when the stones block its path, carving a way forward little by little. As Desmond Tutu said, *"Hope is being able to see that there is light despite all of the darkness."*

Reflection: *What moments in my life have called me to hold on to hope, and how has it carried me through?*

Hope in Everyday Moments

The South teaches us to find hope in the small things—because sometimes, that's all we need to keep moving forward. It is the way the sun warms your face after a storm, the way a friend's smile reminds you that you're not alone, and the way a hymn lifts your spirits even on the hardest days. These fleeting moments of joy remind us that hope often hides in the ordinary.

Consider the elder sitting on her porch, watching as her grandkids play in the yard. The creak of the rocker is her companion, the laughter of the children, her melody. There's hope in the simple beauty of life's rhythms, in the promise that love and laughter endure.

Reflection: *Where can I find hope in my daily life, even amid trials?*

Hope as Resilience

Hope and resilience are intertwined, each feeding the other. It's hope that allows us to face adversity with courage, and it's resilience that ensures hope never fades. The South, with its history of struggle and triumph, teaches us this truth—that hope is not naïve, but bold. It's the belief that things can and will get better, even if the path isn't yet clear.

As Martin Luther King Jr. once said, *"We must accept finite disappointment, but never lose infinite hope."* Hope isn't the absence of struggle; it's the promise of strength within it.

Reflection: *How can hope guide me through life's challenges, and how has resilience helped me hold* on to *it?*

A Reader's Reflection

Let me encourage you to embrace hope.

- *What has hope meant to me in the darkest times of my life, and how has it sustained me?*

- *How can I find hope in the small moments, like the beauty of nature or the kindness of others?*

- *How can hope inspire me to keep moving forward, even when the road feels uncertain?*

The Philosophy of Faith: Rooted and Reaching

Faith runs deep in the South—like the roots of a cypress tree, it anchors lives through storms and seasons. Here, faith isn't just a belief; it's a way of living, a steady heartbeat that echoes in Sunday hymns, evening prayers, and quiet acts of kindness. It's the thread that connects people to something greater than themselves, giving purpose and hope.

Faith is deeply personal, shaped by the experiences and values that guide each individual. It's in the whispers of a parent praying over their child, in the hands clasped together in silent communion, in the song sung not for an audience but for the soul. As Søren Kierkegaard said, "Faith sees *best in the dark.*"

Reflection: *What role does faith play in my life, and how does it guide me in times of uncertainty?*

Faith as Strength

The South teaches that faith isn't a shield to protect us from hardship; it's a source of strength to carry us through it. It's the trust that even when the path is unclear, there's meaning to be found, lessons to be learned, and peace waiting beyond the trial. Faith is the farmer who sows seeds while the drought still lingers, the family who rebuilds after loss, the elder who keeps singing even when the road feels long.

As Martin Luther King Jr. expressed, *"Faith is taking the first step even when you don't see the whole staircase."* Faith is courage—it's stepping forward even when you're uncertain of where the road leads.

Reflection: *How has faith given me the strength to face life's challenges, and what moments in my life have tested its limits?*

Faith as Community

Faith isn't just personal; it's communal, binding people together in shared belief and shared purpose. It's the hand extended in help, the meal offered in kindness, the shoulder given to lean on. Church pews where families gather, hymns rising like a collective prayer, and reminding traditions—all speak to our connection.

Faith builds connection, bringing people together to face challenges as one.

Reflection: *How has faith connected me to others, and how has the strength of community helped me carry my burdens?*

A Reader's Reflection

Let me encourage you to explore your own journey of faith.

- *What does faith mean to me, and how does it guide my choices and my perspective on life?*

- *How has my faith helped me find strength in hard times, and how has it shaped my resilience?*

- *How can faith deepen my connection to others, creating bonds that carry us through life together?*

The Philosophy of Renewal: Turning the Page

Renewal is a promise written into the very fabric of the South, where each season brings its own kind of beginning. Spring bursts forth with wildflowers and blooming magnolias, summer ripens the fields, autumn sheds the old to make way for the new, and winter whispers of rest before the cycle starts again. Renewal isn't just for the land; it's a gift offered to each of us—a chance to start over, to let go, to grow.

The South teaches us to embrace renewal with open arms, much like the way a gardener prunes a plant not to harm it, but to help it thrive. Whether it's a new day dawning after a long night or a new chapter unfolding in the story of our lives, renewal reminds us that the past doesn't have to define the future.

Reflection: *What parts of my life are calling for renewal, and how can I embrace the opportunity to begin again?*

Lessons From the Land

Nature is a gentle teacher when it comes to renewal. Think of the way a field, lying fallow for a season, springs back richer and stronger when the time comes to sow again. Or the way a storm clears the air, leaving the world feeling fresh and alive. The South knows that renewal often follows hardship, like sunlight after rain or peace after struggle.

As F. Scott Fitzgerald once wrote, *"Vitality shows not only in the ability to persist but in the ability to start over."* Renewal isn't about forgetting what came before—it's about honoring it while moving forward.

Reflection: *How can I allow the lessons of my past to shape my renewal, turning old struggles into new strengths?*

Renewal as Growth

Renewal is growth—it's the act of shedding what no longer serves us to make room for something better. It's in the way a tree loses its leaves so it can bud again, stronger and fuller. Renewal invites us to ask the hard questions: *What in my life is ready to be released, and what is waiting to bloom in its place?*

The South reminds us that growth takes time, but it's always worth the wait. Renewal isn't a single moment; it's a journey, a process of transformation that unfolds like seasons turning toward the light.

Reflection: *What steps can I take toward renewal in my life, and how can I nurture the growth that follows?*

A Reader's Reflection

Let me encourage you to embrace renewal in your life:

- *What areas of my life feel ready for a fresh start, and how can I welcome that change?*

- *What lessons from nature's cycles can inspire me to embrace transformation?*

- *How can I see renewal not as an ending, but as a beginning—a chance to grow stronger and thrive?*

Chapter Three Summary: The Tapestry of Life

Chapter Three has been a journey—a winding path through fields of thought, exploring the virtues and values that shape lives both humble and extraordinary. From the seeds we plant in our **Legacies**, to the quiet grace of **Forgiveness**, to the soulful art of **Storytelling**, this chapter reminds us that life is not just a series of moments but a collection of meanings we create and share.

We found wisdom in the stillness of **Solitude**, where reflection reveals truths often overlooked. We listened to the gentle teachings of **Nature**, whose cycles of bloom and fall mirror our own struggles and triumphs. Through the web of **Interconnection**, we saw how our actions ripple outward, binding us to the people and places that shape us in turn.

This chapter invited us to celebrate the small, fleeting moments that bring **Joy**, to embrace the power of **Gratitude** as a lens for abundance, and to marvel at the human spirit's **Resilience** in the face of life's storms. **Hope** anchored us, showing that even in darkness, there was light to guide the way. And through the enduring strength of **Faith**, we found comfort in the belief that something greater than ourselves holds us. Finally, in the promise of **Renewal**, we learned to welcome fresh starts and growth, understanding that every ending carries the seed of a new beginning.

Closing Reflection: The Fabric of Being

As this chapter closes, it's clear singular moments does not define that life but by the rich tapestry they create—a weave of joys and sorrows, beginnings and endings, connections and individuality. Each philosophy explored here is a thread, strong and distinct, but even more beautiful because of the way they intertwine.

To the reader, this chapter is both invitation and inspiration: to live with intention, to find meaning in the ordinary, to weave your own tapestry with love, faith, and hope. For every step taken, every choice made, every connection formed, there is purpose, there is legacy, and there is life abundant.

Chapter Three is a thoughtful exploration of the philosophies that guide and define us, each enriched by timeless words from great thinkers, writers, and leaders:

- **On Legacy:** Friedrich Nietzsche reminds us, *"That which does not kill us makes us stronger,"* showing that the marks we leave behind often come from life's trials.

- **On Forgiveness:** Mahatma Gandhi's wisdom shines

through: *"The weak can never forgive. Forgiveness is the attribute of the strong."*

- **On Storytelling:** Joan Didion beautifully captures the essence: *"We tell ourselves stories in order to live."*

- **On Solitude and Reflection:** Marcus Aurelius grounds us with his timeless truth: *"Nowhere can man find a quieter or more untroubled retreat than in his own soul."*

- **On Nature as a Teacher:** Henry David Thoreau's reverence for life's cycles: *"Live in each season as it passes; breathe the air, drink the drink, taste the fruit, and resign yourself to the influence of the earth."*

- **On Interconnection:** John Donne reminds us, *"No man is an island; every man is a piece of the continent, a part of the main."*

- **On Joy:** Helen Keller's fire of inspiration: *"Joy is the holy fire that keeps our purpose warm and our intelligence aglow."*

- **On Gratitude:** Melody Beattie encapsulates it perfectly: *"Gratitude turns what we have into enough."*

- **On Resilience:** Maya Angelou's strength shines through: *"I can be changed by what happens to me, but I refuse to be reduced by it."*

- **On Hope:** Desmond Tutu offers light in darkness: *"Hope is being able to see that there is light despite all of the darkness."*

- **On Faith:** Søren Kierkegaard provides clarity: *"Faith sees best in the dark."*

- **On Renewal:** F. Scott Fitzgerald inspires growth: *"Vitality shows not only in the ability to persist but in the ability to start over."*

Closing Thought: The Fabric of Being

Life's beauty lies in its complexity, its interconnectedness, and its ability to renew itself. Chapter Three reminds readers to embrace the lessons of legacy, forgiveness, storytelling, solitude, nature, joy, gratitude, resilience, hope, faith, and renewal, weaving these threads together into a tapestry that is uniquely theirs.

Each quote offers a touchstone, a lens through which to view life's wonders and challenges. Together, they inspire readers to live with purpose and intention, to find meaning in the moments both big and small, and to create lives rich with connection and love.

4

Philosophy in Motion

❧

Living Southern Wisdom

Philosophy in Action: Turning Reflection into Practice

The South doesn't just talk about values—it embodies them in ways so subtle, they often feel second nature. Kindness isn't a philosophy discussed over coffee; it's the jar of preserves left on a neighbor's porch, the stranger who fixes your flat tire without asking for thanks. Forgiveness isn't preached in abstract terms; it's the hand extended in reconciliation over a broken fence. Down here, philosophy isn't a topic—it's a way of living.

Take, for instance, Ms. Clara, a retired schoolteacher in a small town where everybody knows everybody. Last spring, a storm rolled through and knocked half the shingles off her neighbor's roof. The neighbor, Mr. Frank, had fallen on hard times, but before he could even figure out how to ask for help, Ms. Clara gathered a small crew of willing hands. Before the sun set, they'd patched that roof so well, it looked like the storm had missed it altogether. When asked why, Ms. Clara just said, *"It needed doing, and that's all there is to it."*

A Quote to Ponder:

"Do not wait; the time will never be 'just right.' Start where you stand, and work with whatever tools you may have at your command."–George

Herbert.

Ms. Clara's story isn't unique—it's echoed in countless small, muted acts across the South, each one a living example of philosophy in action.

Readers might reflect: *What can I do today, however small, to live out the values I hold dear?*

Planting Seeds of Resilience

Mrs. Louisa, an elderly widow, lives at the edge of a small southern town where every field seems to stretch toward forever. Her husband, Henry, passed away two springs ago, leaving her alone with their beloved vegetable garden—a patch of earth that had fed their family and neighbors through good times and bad.

Last summer, a drought hit the town hard. The garden withered, the soil cracked, and the harvest that once overflowed became sparse. Yet Mrs. Louisa didn't give up. With hands worn by decades of labor, she walked to the garden each evening, watering what she could with what she had. As she worked, she hummed a hymn Henry had loved, her voice steady, her heart strong. *"The Lord will provide,"* she whispered as she gently covered the roots with fresh soil.

By autumn, the garden produced just enough—bushels of tomatoes, baskets of okra, bundles of collard greens. Mrs. Louisa didn't keep it all; she handed out what she had to the town's children, saying, *"Take this—it's all grown with hope and a little hymn."*

Memorable Quote:

"Hope is like the sun, which, as we journey toward it, casts the shadow of our burdens behind us."–Samuel Smiles.

Philosophy in Action

Charles E. Cravey

Beneath the sky where the magnolias lean,
Lives a grace so muted, it's often unseen.
In hands that fix, in seeds that sow,
In hearts that heal, in rivers that flow.

Kindness blooms like wildflowers in May,
Forgiveness hums where shadows lay.
Resilience whispers, "Come what will,"
Hope lingers softly yet stands so still.

Life here is woven, not in words alone,
But in casseroles baked and seeds that are grown.
The South lives its wisdom, not loud but true,
In every sunrise and every dew.

The Southern Way of Life: A Lived Philosophy

Life in the South isn't rushed—it's savored, like the first bite of peach cobbler fresh from the oven or the lingering notes of a gospel hymn rising up through an old church's rafters. Down here, values aren't just spoken about; they're lived in the moments that make up a day. It's not uncommon to see philosophy bloom in the rituals of community, connection, and care—each one a small but profound reflection of what it means to live well.

Take Sunday suppers, for instance. There's a magic in those gatherings—a potluck of casseroles, fried chicken, and cornbread, each dish brought with love and a story to tell. Around the table, generations come together—grandparents sharing their wisdom, children their laughter, neighbors their kindness. No one leaves without a full stomach and a fuller heart. It's not just a meal; it's a moment of gratitude, connection, and celebration.

Memorable Quote:

"You don't choose your family. They are God's gift to you, as you are to them."—Desmond Tutu.

In the South, family extends far beyond blood. It's the neighbor who brings over a pitcher of lemonade on a hot day, the friend who drives you to church when your car won't start, the community that gathers to rebuild after a storm. We build life here on the understanding that we are all connected, and that even the smallest acts of care create the biggest difference.

Traditions Rooted in Values

Southern traditions often reflect deeper values—hospitality, kindness, resilience, and faith. Think of the way the front porch becomes a stage for storytelling, a haven for reflection, and a symbol of welcome. Think of the festivals that celebrate everything from peaches to pecans, turning ordinary harvests into extraordinary celebrations.

It's the rhythm of life here that carries philosophy forward, turning routines into rituals and moments into memories.

Readers might reflect: *What traditions in my life reflect my values, and how can I honor them more fully?*

Memorable Quote:

"A people without the knowledge of their history, origin, and culture is like a tree without roots."–Marcus Garvey.

A Southern Snapshot

Picture a small town square on a warm summer evening. The lights are strung between oak trees, casting a golden glow over the gathering crowd. A bluegrass band plays, and within moments, feet are tapping and hands clapping. Neighbors greet each other with smiles and embraces, children dart between legs in a game of tag, and the smell of barbecue wafts through the air. It's not about the music or the food—it's about the community, the connection, the shared joy of simply being together.

Readers might ponder: *How can I bring the spirit of Southern connection into my life, finding joy in the small, shared moments that define us?*

Navigating Life's Crossroads: Choices That Define Us

Life in the South often feels like a series of crossroads—literal dirt paths that meet under the shade of oaks, and metaphorical ones where decisions carry the weight of who we are and who we'll become. The South teaches us to approach these moments not with fear, but with faith and clarity, guided by the philosophies that ground us.

Every choice has ripples, every step a story waiting to unfold. At the heart of it all is the truth that the paths we choose define not just where we go, but who we are.

A Story: The Fork in the Road

Young Will had always known two things: he loved his family's peach orchard, and he dreamed of something more. Raised under the Georgia sun, he'd spent his childhood learning every secret of the trees, every rhythm of the seasons. But when college acceptance letters came in, Will found himself at a crossroads: should he stay and carry on the family legacy, or venture to the city and chase new dreams?

One hot summer evening, Will's grandfather, a man of few words but endless wisdom, sat with him under their oldest peach tree. *"Life's funny,"* his grandfather said, as fireflies lit the twilight. *"The path you take matters, but so does the way you walk it. Stay or go, Will—you'll still be you, and these trees will always welcome you home."*

In that moment, Will realized the crossroads wasn't a test of loyalty, but an invitation to grow. He left—not to escape his roots, but to carry them with him into the world. He'd always return to the orchard, but for now, the road stretched out wide before him, full of possibility.

Memorable Quote:

"In the middle of difficulty lies opportunity."–Albert Einstein.

Readers might reflect: *What crossroads has shaped my life, and how have my choices helped me grow into who I am today?*

The Philosophy of Choice

The South knows choices aren't always clear-cut. Sometimes, the right path isn't the easiest one, but the one that feels true deep down. It's the path that demands courage, asks questions, and pushes you to see beyond the horizon. Whether it's choosing forgiveness over resentment, resilience over despair, or faith over fear, each decision becomes a defining moment.

Readers might ponder: *How do my values guide my decisions, and what legacy do I want my choices to leave behind?*

Memorable Quote:

"You are free to choose, but you are not free from the consequence of your choice."–Southern Proverb.

Building a Legacy of Living Well: Roots and Wings

A legacy isn't just what we leave behind—it's what we nurture while we're here. The South understands this deeply, valuing moments that enrich the soul and connections that endure long after the last hymn is sung. Building a legacy isn't about grandeur; it's about the muted, steady acts that shape lives and hearts. It's about planting seeds not for recognition, but for growth.

A Story: The Quilter's Gift

Grandma Mae had a gift—not just for quilting, but for stitching pieces of history, hope, and love into every square. Over the years, her quilts had warmed countless beds, wrapped crying children, and celebrated new beginnings. But Mae wasn't just making quilts; she was weaving stories. Each patch came with a memory—a scrap from her daughter's prom dress, a piece of her husband's old flannel, the corner of a tablecloth from the church picnic.

One autumn, Mae created something special: a quilt for the community. She worked tirelessly, collecting fabrics from neighbors, friends, and strangers. Each piece told a story, and Mae stitched them together with care. When the quilt was finished, it became the centerpiece of the town's harvest festival—a beautiful mosaic of lives intertwined. Mae's legacy wasn't just the quilt—it was the love she poured into every thread, the connections she fostered, and the stories she helped others remember.

Memorable Quote:

"What we do for ourselves dies with us. What we do for others and the world remains and is immortal."–Albert Pike.

Readers might reflect: *What pieces of my life am I stitching into a legacy, and how can I ensure those pieces carry love, meaning, and connection?*

Living the Legacy Now

Legacy isn't about the future—it's about the present, about living in ways that enrich our own lives and those of others. It's the farmer who shares his best peaches at church, the teacher who inspires her students to dream bigger, the elder who passes down family stories by the fireplace. These moments of generosity, care, and wisdom create ripples that will be felt long after they've passed.

Readers might ponder: *How can I live today in a way that creates moments worth remembering, connections worth cherishing, and values worth passing on?*

Memorable Quote:

"Carve your name on hearts, not tombstones. A legacy is etched into the minds of others and the stories they share about you."–Shannon L. Alder.

A Southern Snapshot: Roots and Wings

Imagine a small family reunion on a warm summer evening. Under the shade of a magnolia tree, laughter flows like the breeze. The elder of the family, Uncle Joe, sits in his rocking chair with a Bible on his lap and a tale to tell. He shares the story of how he built their family's cabin by hand, with only determination and borrowed tools. The children listen wide-eyed, and the adults smile, knowing they'll carry Joe's grit and wisdom into their own lives. His legacy isn't just the cabin—it's the spirit of resilience and love he's passed down.

Chapter Conclusion: A Life Well Lived

As the sun sets on this chapter, it leaves behind the glow of lives lived with purpose and connection. In the South, wisdom isn't just found in words—it's found in actions, in traditions, in the love that ties people together like patchwork quilts or the roots of ancient trees.

From choosing kindness at every crossroads to savoring the richness of shared moments, this chapter reminds us that life's greatest philosophies don't belong on dusty shelves or in lofty debates. They belong in the soft drawl of a grandmother's voice, in the steady rhythm of a farmer's hands, in the echo of a hymn sung under starlight.

The legacy of Southern wisdom isn't about what we leave behind—it's about how we live right now. It's about building something lasting in the hearts of others, about choosing hope over despair, about seeing life not as a race to the finish, but as a journey worth treasuring every step of the way.

5

The Bridge Forward

As the world turns faster and progress reshapes every corner, the South stands as both a witness to change and a keeper of timeless truths. Wisdom here doesn't resist the future—it embraces it while holding onto the values that anchor us. Chapter Five is about the journey forward, where the legacy of tradition meets the opportunities of tomorrow, and where wisdom evolves to guide us into the unknown.

Carrying Stories Across Generations

The art of storytelling, so central to Southern life, becomes a bridge across time. As modern technology changes the ways we communicate, oral traditions adapt and thrive, finding new platforms without losing their soul. Shared tales of resilience, hope, and connection—once told on front porches—now find their way into podcasts, digital diaries, and virtual gatherings. The key is not what changes, but what remains: the heart of the stories themselves.

Memorable Quote:

"Stories are the communal currency of humanity."–Tahir Shah.

To pass on stories is to pass on identity, ensuring that the lessons of those who came before continue to shape those who will come after.

Readers might reflect: *How can I share the wisdom I've received with others, ensuring it grows and evolves with the times?*

Balancing Tradition with Progress

The South has always cherished its traditions—meals shared, hymns sung, fields tended with care. But it also knows that progress is necessary, a call to adapt, innovate, and embrace the challenges and opportunities that lie ahead. The balance isn't about choosing one over the other; it's about blending them into a harmonious whole.

Memorable Quote:

"Tradition is not the worship of ashes, but the preservation of fire."–Gustav Mahler.

Consider the farmer who uses cutting-edge technology to enhance his crops while still honoring the rituals of harvest celebrated by generations before him. Progress isn't an abandonment of the past; it's a continuation of its spirit, expressed in new and meaningful ways.

Readers might ponder: *How can I balance tradition with progress in my life, ensuring each enhances the other?*

Hope for Tomorrow: Shaping the Future Together

If the philosophies of resilience, gratitude, and faith have taught us anything, it's that hope is not just a personal virtue—it's a communal act. The South knows that tomorrow is built not by individuals working alone, but by communities coming together with shared purpose and determination.

Memorable Quote:

"The best way to predict the future is to create it."–Peter Drucker.

From neighbors rebuilding homes after storms to families planting trees they'll never live to see grow tall. Hope takes root in acts of care and connection.

Readers might reflect: *What can I do today to nurture hope—not just for myself, but for my community and the world beyond?*

Wisdom as a Continuum

The beauty of Southern wisdom lies in its ability to evolve. It's not stagnant; it adapts, grows, and thrives in the hearts of each new generation. What remains constant is its essence—a deep respect for the land, the people, and the stories that tie them together. We carry forward wisdom not as an unchanging relic, but as a living, breathing truth that takes on new shapes as we share it.

Memorable Quote:

"There is a continuity in the wisdom of the past and the possibilities of the future. They are not separate—they are intertwined."-Anonymous.

Readers might wonder: *What wisdom do I carry I can pass on in ways that resonate with both the past and the future?*

The Future Rooted in the Past

The South knows that roots hold the strength of the tree, yet it also knows that the tree must stretch toward the sky. As time moves forward, the wisdom carried through generations becomes a guide—not as a tether to hold us back, but as a foundation upon which we build the future. This chapter celebrates that balance: standing strong in tradition while embracing the unknown with open arms.

Imagine a young artist named Ellie, raised in the same small southern town her family has called home for five generations. The stories sparked Ellie's love for painting her grandmother told her on summer evenings—tales of resilience, love, and triumph woven through the town's history. As Ellie grew older, she found new ways to express those stories, blending traditional Southern imagery with modern techniques that defy conventions. Some folks resisted her bold style, calling it too modern, but Ellie knew that honoring tradition didn't mean recreating it; it meant letting it inspire her to create something new.

Ellie's work soon caught the attention of galleries across the country, but she always stayed rooted in the South. When asked what inspired her, she said, *"It's the people, the stories, the land itself. I'm not just painting for me—I'm painting for those who came before and those who will come after."*

Memorable Quote:

"The past is not dead. It's not even past."–William Faulkner.

Wisdom Growing Through Challenges

The South has faced its share of challenges, from the scars of history to the storms of nature. Yet each challenge has been a teacher, shaping a wisdom that is both humble and resilient. The future doesn't ask us to forget those lessons; it asks us to carry them forward in ways that heal, grow, and unite.

Consider the words of Maya Angelou: *"History, despite its wrenching pain, cannot be unlived, but if faced with courage, need not be lived again."*

Readers might ponder: *How can I take the lessons of my history and use them to build a stronger, brighter future—for myself and for those around me?*

The Continuum of Southern Wisdom

One of the most beautiful truths about wisdom is that it doesn't end—it evolves, flowing like a river that shapes the land it touches.

Southern wisdom, grounded in resilience, gratitude, and faith, grows richer with every generation that takes it up and makes it their own.

The South teaches us that the greatest legacies aren't written in stone; they're written in hearts, in actions, in the way we live and love. And as this wisdom moves forward, it carries the promise that every story told, every act of kindness, and every moment of courage will ripple outward, touching lives yet to come.

Memorable Quote:

"We are made wise not by the recollection of our past, but by the responsibility for our future."—George Bernard Shaw.

The Power of Small Actions

The South teaches us it's not always the grand gestures that define a life well lived; often, it's the small, everyday acts of care that carry the greatest weight. These acts, though humble in scale, have a way of creating ripples that extend far beyond their moment, touching lives in ways we may never fully see.

Consider the small-town librarian who stays late to teach a teenager how to write a college essay, or the farmer who sets aside the first box of peaches for the family next door because he knows they've been struggling. These aren't acts performed for glory—they're simply part of a life lived with intention, where kindness isn't an exception but a rule.

Memorable Quote:

"Great things are not done by impulse, but by a series of small things brought together."–Vincent Van Gogh.

Readers might reflect: *What small actions can I take today to live out my values and create ripples of kindness and connection?*

A Reflection on Shared Responsibility

The future isn't built by one person; it's shaped by the collective actions of many. The South knows this well, with its history of neighbors stepping in for one another, communities rallying after storms, and families leaning on each other during hard times. Every act of care, no matter how small, contributes to the whole, creating a brighter, more connected tomorrow.

Memorable Quote:

"Alone we can do so little; together we can do so much."–Helen Keller.

When we recognize the power of shared responsibility, we begin to see that our actions are not just for ourselves—they are for everyone around us.

Readers might ask: *How can I contribute to the collective good, creating a legacy of connection and care?*

A vision for the future is taking shape: one built not on perfection or grandeur, but on intention, action, and a deep understanding of our interconnectedness. Southern wisdom reminds us that every sunrise brings an opportunity to plant seeds—of kindness, hope, resilience, and love—each one carrying the promise of a brighter tomorrow.

A Unified Vision: Shaping Tomorrow Together

As we move forward, the South reminds us of a truth both simple and profound: the future isn't an isolated venture—it's a shared journey. In every field tended, every story told, every act of care extended, there's a ripple that reaches far beyond the present. Together, these ripples shape the continuum of wisdom, ensuring that the values we hold dear don't just survive, but thrive.

Take the story of Mr. Samuels, the town's oldest living resident. At 92, his hands are as weathered as the plow he once used to till his family's farm, but his spirit remains bright. Each spring, Mr. Samuels gathers the town's children under the old pecan tree to teach them about planting. He tells stories about the land, about resilience and hope, about how "every seed carries a promise." What starts as a lesson about farming becomes a lesson about life—a reminder that the future isn't built by one generation alone, but by the collective effort of many.

The children grow older, and Mr. Samuels' pecan tree becomes a gathering place where they pass down his wisdom. The seeds they plant don't just nourish the soil—they nourish the spirit, each one a testament to the power of shared vision and care.

Memorable Quote:

"The best way to find yourself is to lose yourself in the service of other s."–Mahatma Gandhi.

Readers might reflect: *How can I contribute to a shared future, ensuring that my actions create ripples of hope and connection for generations to come?*

Harmony Between the Old and the New

The South knows that progress isn't an erasure of tradition—it's an extension of it, a way to ensure its spirit lives on in new forms. Just as rivers carve new paths while carrying the same water, the philosophies of the past find fresh expressions in the hands of each new generation.

Picture a modern-day architect designing a community center. Inspired by the town's rich history, she incorporates materials salvaged from the old train depot and features that mimic the design of the oldest church in the county. Yet the center is equipped with solar panels and spaces for digital learning. Her work blends the old and the new into a seamless whole, honoring the past while preparing for the future.

Memorable Quote:

"The art of progress is to preserve order amid change, and to preserve change amid order."–Alfred North Whitehead.

Readers might ponder: *How can I honor the past while creating space for progress, blending tradition with innovation in ways that enhance both?*

Chapter Five invites readers to embrace a vision of tomorrow where wisdom is not just preserved but transformed into new possibilities. It's a reminder that the values of resilience, gratitude, faith, and hope are not relics—they are tools for shaping the future, for building communities that are both rooted and reaching.

Every sunrise carries the promise of renewal, every act of kindness plants seeds of hope, every shared story strengthens the ties that bind us. The bridge forward isn't just about moving ahead—it's about carrying the essence of what makes life meaningful into every step we take.

Closing Reflection—Carrying the Light Forward

As the bridge forward unfolds, we carry with us the wisdom of the past, the resilience of the present, and the hope of the future. The south teaches us that life's most profound philosophies aren't meant to stand still—they are meant to move, to grow, to shape the world we share.

This chapter celebrates the continuum of wisdom, where every act of care, every seed of kindness, and every story told becomes a part of something greater. It reminds us that the future isn't something distant and unreachable—it begins with each sunrise, each small action, each connection forged.

We leave Chapter Five with this truth: the legacy of living well isn't written in stone, but in the hearts and hands of those willing to carry it forward. And as we step into the future, may we do so with gratitude for where we've been, faith in where we're going, and a shared commitment to building a world rich with meaning, connection, and love.

6

The Heart of Purpose

❧

Living With Intention

Finding Purpose in the Everyday

The South teaches us that purpose isn't always found in monumental achievements; often, it blooms in the quiet rhythm of daily life. Tending a garden, baking biscuits for Sunday supper, sharing a laugh with a neighbor—all these moments carry meaning when approached with intention and care.

Consider Miss Evelyn, the town baker who rises before dawn each day to make her famous pecan pies. For her, baking isn't just a routine—it's her way of spreading joy. Each pie holds a little love and a little legacy, passed from her grandmother's recipe to the hands of strangers who savor every bite. When asked why she does it, Miss Evelyn says simply, *"Because a sweet pie can make the bitter days easier to bear."*

Memorable Quote:

"To find joy in work is to discover the fountain of youth."–Pearl S. Buck.

Purpose in the everyday reminds us that even the smallest acts—planting a seed, offering a smile—can be profound when done with intention.

Readers might reflect: *How can I bring purpose to the ordinary moments of* my life, *turning routines into rituals and tasks into treasures?*

The Heart of Purpose

Charles E. Cravey

Beneath the arc of Southern skies,
Where whispers weave through fireflies,
There lies a rhythm, soft and true,
A muted call in all we do.

In gardens green and kitchens warm,
In kindness shared through storm and calm,
The heart of purpose hums its tune,
In morning's glow and evening's moon.

It's found in work, in love, in rest,
In hands that give, in hearts that bless.
Not grand, nor loud, yet still profound,
It roots our souls; it holds us bound.

A table set, a story told,
A child's hand in a father's hold—
Each fleeting moment, rich in grace,
A sacred step, a timeless space.

Oh, South, you teach through soil and song,
That purpose found will carry on.
Not bound by time, yet here to stay,
In every life, in every day.

The Courage to Seek Purpose

Finding purpose isn't always easy. It requires introspection, vulnerability, and the willingness to venture into the unknown. The South reminds us that courage isn't about being fearless—it's about stepping forward even when the road ahead seems uncertain.

Take the story of young Clara. Raised in a small Southern town, she always felt drawn to music, but lacked the confidence to pursue it. One summer evening, she attended the county fair, where the main stage was set for a singing competition. Clara sat in the back, heart pounding as she listened to contestant after contestant. Just as the emcee called for the final entrant, Clara felt something stir within her—a muted voice urging her forward.

With trembling hands, she made her way to the stage. Her voice shook at first, but as she sang, her confidence grew. By the final verse, the crowd was on its feet, cheering for the girl who had found her voice. Clara didn't win the contest, but she left with something far more valuable: the courage to pursue her dream of music.

Memorable Quote:

"It takes courage to grow up and become who you really are."–E. E. Cummings.

Readers might reflect: *What areas of my life are calling for courage, and how can I take the first step toward discovering my own purpose?*

Seeking with Resilience

The South knows that finding purpose isn't a straight path—it's full of twists, turns, and trials. But it also teaches that resilience is the key to forging ahead.

Readers might ask: *When the journey feels hard, what strengths can I draw upon to keep moving forward?*

Memorable Quote:

"Courage is not having the strength to go on; it is going on when you don't have the strength."–Theodore Roosevelt.

Purpose as Connection

Purpose isn't solitary; it's born and nurtured through the relationships we build and the communities we shape. The South is a master of connection, teaching us that when we live with intention, we extend our purpose outward—not just for ourselves, but for others.

Imagine Mr. Nathaniel, the mailman who's more than just a carrier of letters. Every morning, he makes his rounds across town, but his purpose isn't just delivering envelopes—it's delivering smiles, encouragement, and care. He knows everyone's names, their birthdays, their joys, and their struggles. When someone faces hard times, Mr. Nathaniel is the first to rally support, turning mailboxes into bridges of connection. His purpose lies in the kindness he carries, reminding us all that even the simplest roles hold the potential for profound impact.

Memorable Quote:

"What is the essence of life? To serve others and to do good."–Aristotle.

Readers might reflect: *How can I extend my purpose outward, using it to strengthen connections and build communities rich with care and meaning?*

The Ripple Effect of Intention

The beauty of purpose as connection lies in the ripples it creates. A single act of care—a casserole brought to a grieving neighbor, a porch conversation that lifts someone's spirits, a hand extended in forgiveness—can inspire others to do the same. The South reminds us that purpose isn't about what we achieve alone; it's about the legacy of love and care we leave behind in the lives we touch.

Memorable Quote:

"When we give cheerfully and accept gratefully, everyone is blessed." –Maya Angelou.

Readers might ask: *What ripples am I creating through my connections, and how can I live with intention to ensure those ripples carry hope, joy, and strength to others?*

Purpose as a Legacy

A legacy isn't built in grand gestures or sweeping achievements; it's woven quietly in the everyday acts of care and intention that touch lives and leave lasting impressions. The South teaches us that purpose is not just about living well in the present—it's about creating ripples that extend into the future, shaping hearts and communities long after the last chapter closes.

Take the story of Reverend Hayes, who spent his life serving a small rural church tucked into the Carolina hills. Reverend Hayes wasn't famous; he didn't write books or give televised sermons. But his weekly messages of hope, faith, and resilience became the foundation for a community that thrived in the face of storms, struggles, and change. Years after his passing, the church walls still echo with his words, and the children he baptized carry his wisdom as they raise their own families. His purpose was simple yet profound: to nurture a legacy of love and faith that transcends time.

Memorable Quote:

"The great use of life is to spend it for something that will outlast it."–William James.

Readers might reflect: *How can I live in ways that create a legacy of connection, kindness, and meaning for the generations to come?*

The Seeds We Plant

Legacy isn't just about what we leave behind; it's about the seeds we plant every day—seeds of hope, strength, and joy that take root and flourish in the lives of others. The South knows the beauty of small, intentional acts, whether it's the farmer who teaches his grandchildren to sow crops with care or the teacher who inspires students to see their own potential.

Memorable Quote:

"Someone is sitting in the shade today because someone planted a tree a long time ago."–Warren Buffett.

Readers might ponder: *What seeds am I planting through my daily actions, and how will they shape the world for those who follow?*

Legacy as Connection

Ultimately, purpose as a legacy is about connection—about recognizing that every choice, every act, every word carries the potential to touch lives beyond our own. When we live with intention, we create a mosaic of meaning that strengthens the bonds between individuals, families, and communities.

Memorable Quote:

"Your legacy is every life you've ever touched."–Maya Angelou.

Chapter Six: Closing Reflection—The Light of Purpose

As we step out of Chapter Six, we carry with us the wisdom of living with intention—a reminder that purpose isn't always found in the extraordinary; it's often found in the small, muted moments where meaning takes root. Whether through courage, connection, or legacy, purpose guides us to live lives that resonate deeply, both within ourselves and outward into the world.

The South teaches us that purpose is not just a destination—it's a way of being, woven into the fabric of daily life. It reminds us to savor each sunrise, embrace each challenge, and nurture each relationship with care and intention. When we live with purpose, we create ripples that extend far beyond our own lives, shaping a legacy rich with meaning, connection, and hope.

As we leave this chapter, may we carry its truths into the days ahead: to seek purpose with courage, to find it in the everyday, to share it through connection, and to build it into a legacy that endures. For in every small act, every choice made with intention, we find the heart of purpose—a light that guides us forward.

7

The Wisdom of Seasons

Life moves in seasons, each bringing its own rhythms, challenges, and gifts. The South, with its deep connection to the cycles of nature, teaches us to embrace these changes as opportunities for growth and reflection. Whether it's the renewal of spring, the abundance of summer, the letting go of autumn, or the muted rest of winter, every season offers wisdom to carry forward.

Theme 1: Growth in Spring

Spring reminds us that beginnings are beautiful, even when they are uncertain. It's the season of growth, where seeds take root and possibilities bloom. Just as the land awakens after winter's rest, so do we find ourselves awakening to new opportunities and directions.

Take the story of Mr. Parsons, a retired professor who turned his backyard into a community garden. Each spring, he invites neighbors to join him in planting vegetables and flowers. The garden becomes more than just a place to grow food—it becomes a space to cultivate connection, hope, and renewal. As the seeds sprout, so do friendships and dreams.

Memorable Quote:

"Every spring is the only spring—a perpetual astonishment."–Ellis

Peters.

Readers might reflect: *What seeds am I planting in my own life, and how can I nurture them into growth?*

Theme 2: Abundance in Summer

Summer is the season of abundance and celebration. It reminds us to savor life's richness, to gather together, and to bask in the rewards of our efforts. Whether it's a porch supper shared with loved ones or a festival under the stars, summer teaches us to embrace joy and gratitude.

Memorable Quote:

"What good is the warmth of summer, without the cold of winter to give it sweetness?"–John Steinbeck.

Readers might ponder: *How can I celebrate the abundance in my life, honoring the moments that bring joy and connection?*

Theme 3: Autumn's Lessons of Letting Go

Autumn teaches us the beauty of release—the season when trees shed their leaves, preparing for renewal. In life, letting go can be difficult, yet it's necessary to make space for growth, change, and new beginnings. The South, with its fields of turning gold and scarlet, reminds us that letting go isn't an end—it's a transformation.

Consider Mrs. Hattie, who had lived in the same farmhouse for over forty years. When her children grew up and moved away, she realized it was time to downsize. Though the decision was bittersweet, she approached it with grace, donating family heirlooms to the local museum and sharing her harvest tools with younger farmers in the community. With each step of letting go, Mrs. Hattie found herself lighter, freer, and ready for the next season of her life.

Memorable Quote:

"Life starts all over again when it gets crisp in the fall."–F. Scott Fitzgerald.

Readers might reflect: *What am I holding onto that I need to release, and how can letting go create space for something new?*

Theme 4: Winter's Rest and Reflection

Winter reminds us of the importance of rest—a season of stillness, where the land sleeps and prepares for renewal. In life, we often forget to pause, to reflect, and to rejuvenate. The South, with its quiet winters of frost-kissed fields and warm firesides, offers a gentle reminder: rest is not a luxury—it's a necessity.

Think of Mr. Howard, a lifelong fisher who takes the winter months to mend his nets, reflect on the year gone by, and plan for the seasons ahead. His fireside evenings aren't idle; they're rich with meaning, as he remembers lessons from the water, celebrates his blessings, and sets intentions for the spring. By embracing rest, Mr. Howard finds himself ready to face the next journey with clarity and strength.

Memorable Quote:

"In the depths of winter, I finally learned that within me there lay an invincible summer."–Albert Camus.

Readers might ponder: *How can I make space for rest and reflection in my life, embracing the quiet moments as opportunities for renewal?*

A Reflection on the Wisdom of Seasons

As we move through the seasons of life, we find meaning not in resisting change, but in embracing its lessons. Spring invites growth, summer abundance, autumn transformation, and winter rest. Together, they create a cycle of renewal, reminding us that every ending carries the promise of a new beginning.

Final Reflection: Embracing Life's Seasons

Life moves like the tides, the seasons, the rhythm of a slow southern drawl—steady, profound, and meaningful. Each season carries its wisdom, asking us not to resist its gifts but to embrace them. Spring teaches us to grow, summer to celebrate, autumn to release, and winter to rest. Together, they form a mosaic of change and renewal, reminding us that every chapter of life, no matter how fleeting, serves a purpose.

As we navigate our own seasons, may we do so with gratitude for the lessons they bring and the cycles they complete. For just as the land follows the rhythm of nature, so do our lives, forever turning, forever renewing, forever moving toward what's next.

Wisdom of Seasons

Charles E. Cravey

The Beneath the sky where magnolias sway.
The seasons call in their timeless way.
Spring whispers hope, a budding bloom,
Summer sings life in its golden plume.

Autumn lets go, in hues aflame.
Winter stands still, yet never the same.
Each one a teacher, muted yet clear,
Guiding us onward through every year.

From springtime's promise to winter's rest,
Each season reminds us, life's at its best—
Not in the rushing, but in the flow,

In growing, and changing, and letting go.

Oh, South, you teach through sun and rain,
That life will always rise again.
For just as the soil yields to the sky,
So do our spirits learn to fly.

8

Grace and Gratitude

G race and gratitude—two muted forces that hold immense power. The South, with its traditions of hospitality and its enduring faith, teaches us to embrace these virtues as cornerstones of a life well lived. Whether shown in moments of struggle, forgiveness, celebration, or reflection, grace and gratitude can transform our relationships, our communities, and ourselves.

Theme 1: Gratitude as a Way of Seeing the World

Gratitude isn't just an occasional thank-you; it's a way of perceiving life through the lens of abundance and appreciation. The South teaches us to find joy in life's simplest blessings—a glass of sweet tea on a warm day, the sound of crickets at dusk, a meal shared with loved ones. Gratitude shifts our focus from what we lack to what we have, nurturing contentment and peace.

Consider Miss Lorraine, the town's unofficial "thank-you note writer." Every month, she sits down with her collection of notecards to express gratitude to those who've touched her life. From the mechanic who fixed her car to the neighbor who shared a casserole, Miss Lorraine's heartfelt notes remind everyone that no act of kindness is too small to be acknowledged. Her gratitude becomes a ripple, spreading warmth and connection throughout the town.

Memorable Quote:

"Gratitude turns what we have into enough."–Anonymous.

Readers might reflect: *What simple blessings in my life can I celebrate with gratitude, and how can I share that gratitude with others?*

The Practice of Grace: Moments of Forgiveness and Understanding

Grace is often described as unearned favor—a silent power that transforms hearts and builds bridges where divisions once stood. In the South, grace is seen not just in words, but in actions: a neighbor mending fences after a quarrel, a family welcoming a stranger at their table, a church congregation opening its doors to those in need. Grace reminds us that to forgive, to understand, and to extend kindness is to invite healing into our lives and the lives of others.

Take the story of Sarah and her father, Mr. Carter. Years ago, a misunderstanding had driven a wedge between them. For years, they exchanged only brief, tense phone calls on holidays. But one Christmas, Sarah mustered the courage to visit him unannounced. She brought a homemade pecan pie—his favorite—and simply said, *"I'd like to start again."* Her father, at first silent, finally nodded, his eyes softening. Over that shared pie, decades of pain melted away, replaced by grace and understanding. Their relationship didn't just heal—it flourished.

Memorable Quote:

"Grace means that all of your mistakes now serve a purpose instead of serving shame."–Brené Brown.

Grace in the Face of Struggles

Grace doesn't always come easily. In moments of hardship, it requires a strength that feels beyond us—a willingness to choose compassion over anger, hope over despair. Yet, it's in these very moments that grace shines brightest, offering us a path toward peace.

Readers might reflect: *How can I practice grace when faced with struggles or misunderstandings, allowing it to bring healing and unity?*

Memorable Quote:

"The weak can never forgive. Forgiveness is the attribute of the strong."–Mahatma Gandhi.

Finding Joy in Life's Simple Blessings

In the rush of daily life, it's easy to overlook the small, muted joys that surround us. But the South, with its porch swings, family gatherings, and warm conversations, reminds us that true happiness often lies in the ordinary moments that weave our days together. Finding joy isn't about chasing grand experiences—it's about savoring life's simple blessings with an open heart.

Consider the story of Mrs. Belle, a widow who finds her greatest joy in watching the sunrise each morning from her rocking chair. With a cup of coffee in hand, she listens to the world wake up—the chirping of birds, the rustle of leaves, the distant sound of a train. For Mrs. Belle, each sunrise is a reminder that every day is a gift, filled with beauty and possibility. Her muted ritual inspires those around her to slow down and find their own moments of gratitude.

Memorable Quote:

"Enjoy the little things, for one day you may look back and realize they were the big things."–Robert Brault.

Readers might reflect: *What simple moments in my life bring me joy, and how can I be more intentional in cherishing them?*

The Southern Art of Celebration

The South knows how to celebrate life's blessings, whether it's a backyard barbecue, a Sunday hymn, or a spontaneous dance under the stars. These moments of joy are not about extravagance—they're about connection, gratitude, and the shared experience of being alive. Readers might ask: *How can I create space for celebration in my life, honoring the beauty of connection and community?*

Memorable Quote:

"Happiness is not a goal; it is a by-product."–Eleanor Roosevelt.

Final Reflection: The Power of Grace and Gratitude

As this chapter concludes, we carry with us the muted yet profound truth that grace and gratitude have the power to transform not just our lives, but the lives of those we touch. Grace teaches us to forgive, to embrace understanding, and to extend kindness without expectation. Gratitude shifts our focus to the abundance that surrounds us, creating a life rich with contentment and joy.

The South, with its traditions of hospitality and connection, reminds us that these virtues are not just practices—they are ways of being, woven into the fabric of everyday life. When we live with grace and gratitude, we open ourselves to deeper relationships, greater resilience, and a profound sense of purpose.

May we carry the lessons of grace and gratitude into the days ahead, finding beauty in life's simple blessings, offering understanding in moments of struggle, and celebrating the connections that make life meaningful.

Grace and Gratitude

Charles E. Cravey

Grace flows soft like Southern rain.
Healing hearts and easing pain.
It whispers calmly, extends its hand,
A bridge of peace where none may stand.

Gratitude hums a steady song.
It fills the day; it makes us strong.
A sunrise kiss, a porch light glow,
A muted joy we come to know.

Together, they dance like fireflies bright.
Lighting the world with their muted might.
Through every season, storm, or sun,
They guide us gently, one by one.

Oh, South, you cradle these truths so well,
In every story, in every tale.
For grace and gratitude, timeless and true,
Are gifts that live in me and you.

9

The Light Within

Within every soul lies a light—a muted, steadfast presence that illuminates even the darkest paths. The South, with its deep sense of faith, resilience, and connection to both community and solitude, teaches us the importance of tending to this inner light. It's a light born of reflection, nurtured by belief, and carried forward by hope.

Theme 1: Cultivating Inner Strength

Life is full of challenges that test our resolve, yet it's in these moments that we discover the depth of our inner strength. The South reminds us that resilience isn't about enduring hardship—it's about rising above it, stronger and more compassionate than before.

Take the story of Ella Mae, a young woman who faced loss early in life. After a hurricane destroyed her family's home, she began rebuilding piece by piece, brick by brick. With every swing of the hammer, she reminded herself that her strength wasn't just in her hands, but in her heart. She leaned on her faith, found support in her neighbors, and discovered a wellspring of resilience she hadn't known she possessed.

Memorable Quote:

"She stood in the storm, and when the wind did not blow her way, she

adjusted her sails."–Elizabeth Edwards.

Readers might reflect: *How can I cultivate my inner strength, allowing it to guide me through life's challenges with courage and grace?*

Theme 2: Faith as an Anchor in Uncertain Times

In life's storms, faith is the anchor that holds us steady. The South, with its enduring traditions of spirituality and resilience, reminds us that faith isn't just about belief—it's about trust, hope, and finding strength in what we cannot always see.

Consider James, a young father who faced a period of unemployment that left him unsure of how to provide for his family. Amid his struggles, he found solace in his faith, often reading Psalms in the evening's quiet while his children slept. With each verse, he felt a muted reassurance that no matter how uncertain the road; he wasn't walking it alone. His faith gave him the courage to keep searching, and eventually, he found a new job that not only supported his family, but reignited his sense of purpose.

Memorable Quote:

"Faith is taking the first step even when you don't see the whole stair case."–Martin Luther King Jr.

Faith as a Source of Hope: Faith isn't always tied to religion—it can also encompass believing in better days ahead, the conviction that kindness is powerful or trusting that one can find meaning even in difficulty. The South teaches us to lean into hope, whether it's through the steady cadence of a hymn, the comfort of a neighbor's embrace, or the resilience of the land itself.

Readers might ask: *What anchors me when the waters of life feel uncertain, and how can I nurture that faith to carry me forward?*

Memorable Quote:

"Faith sees the invisible, believes the unbelievable, and receives the impossible."–Corrie ten Boom.

Theme 3: Finding Joy and Strength in Solitude and Reflection

In a world that often rushes forward, the South teaches us the value of pausing—of finding joy and strength in solitude and the stillness it offers. Whether it's an evening on the porch with nothing but the sound of cicadas, or a walk-through fields kissed by morning dew, reflection creates a space where we reconnect with ourselves and redis-cover the light within.

Anna Louise, a potter with a heart as earthy as her clay, finds her truest self within the quiet solitude of her studio. Sunlight streams through the open window, illuminating dust mites dancing in the air and casting warm light on the wheel where she spends her days.

Her hands, perpetually stained a warm ochre, move with practiced grace, coaxing life from shapeless lumps of clay. The only sounds are the rhythmic whir of the potter's wheel, a gentle sigh as the clay yields to her touch, and the chirping of birds outside, a sweet counterpoint to the intense focus within.

These moments of creation are not just about shaping clay; they are a meditation, a journey inward. She reflects on the challenges she's faced – the early struggles to find her artistic voice, the criticism that stung, the moments of self-doubt that threatened to overwhelm her. But she also savors her triumphs – the first piece she was truly proud of, the recognition from fellow artists, the satisfaction of seeing her work bring joy to others. Her hopes for the future – a solo exhibition, a commission for a prestigious gallery, the feeling of complete creative fulfillment–dance in her mind alongside the memories.

The solitude isn't loneliness; it's a sanctuary, a space where she can connect with her deepest self, shedding the noise of the outside world to find the calm clarity that fuels her art.

In the muted hum of her studio, she discovers a profound sense of peace, a feeling of being wholly present and utterly alive. It is this peace, this centeredness, which infuses her pottery with a unique richness, a depth of meaning that transcends mere aesthetics.

Her pieces are not just beautiful objects; they are vessels filled with the beauty she has found within herself, in the quiet heart of her creative sanctuary.

Memorable Quote:

"Silence is the sleep that nourishes wisdom."–Francis Bacon.

The Transformative Power of Reflection

Reflection allows us to step back, to pause, and to see life from a clearer perspective. It's in these moments of stillness that we find strength to face challenges, gratitude for life's blessings, and hope for what lies ahead. The South reminds us that reflection isn't a retreat—it's a powerful act of renewal.

Readers might ask: *How can I make space for solitude and reflection in my life, allowing it to nurture my inner light?*

Memorable Quote:

"Within you there is a stillness and a sanctuary to which you can retreat at any time and be yourself."–Hermann Hesse.

Final Reflection: Tending the Light Within

The light within each of us is both fragile and powerful. It's the quiet strength that carries us through challenges, the unwavering faith that steadies us in uncertainty, and the inner joy that sparks even in solitude. The South teaches us that this light is not something we seek outside ourselves—it's something we nurture within, through resilience, reflection, and hope.

As this chapter closes, we are reminded that tending to this inner light is not just a gift to ourselves, but to the world. A heart illuminated with strength and faith becomes a beacon for others, spreading warmth, guidance, and connection. May we carry this light forward, allowing it to shine in the smallest moments and the greatest challenges.

The Light Within

Charles E. Cravey

Beneath the pines and twilight's glow,
There lives a light we come to know.
It flickers soft, yet steady stays.
A faithful guide through winding ways.

In storms it whispers, calm and sure,
A beacon bright, a force so pure.
Through solitude, it softly hums,
A song of strength as morning comes.

Oh, South, your wisdom tends this flame,
In faith, in hope, it burns the same.
A legacy of muted grace,
A radiant light in every space.

So, tend this spark, this light inside,
With courage strong, let it abide.

For when the world feels dark and thin,
It shines—the endless light within.

10

A Life Well Lived

What does it mean to live a life well lived? The question itself evokes a sense of contemplation, a yearning for understanding the essence of a fulfilling existence. The American South, with its rich tapestry of enduring traditions and deeply rooted values, offers an interesting perspective. It suggests that the pursuit of a life well lived isn't defined by the relentless striving for flawless perfection or the accumulation of material grandeur. Instead, it hinges on a more profound and nuanced understanding: living authentically, embracing gratitude, and cultivating a deep sense of purpose. This isn't merely a passive existence; it's an active engagement with life. It involves cherishing each precious moment, however fleeting, nurturing and honoring each meaningful connection forged with others, and imbuing every action, no matter how seemingly insignificant, with intention and meaning.

This mindful approach transforms daily life into a tapestry woven with threads of gratitude, authenticity, and purposeful action, contributing to a life rich in meaning and satisfaction. The Southern ethos teaches us that true fulfillment comes not from external achievements, but from the inner richness we cultivate through conscious living.

Theme 1: Reflections on Wisdom Gained

As we look back on the path we've traveled, we find that wisdom isn't born of ease—it's shaped by experience, growth, and resilience. The South teaches us to hold this wisdom close, using it to guide our choices and inspire the lives of those around us.

Henry, a retired carpenter with hands weathered by years of dedicated work, spends his peaceful afternoons under the shade of his beloved oak tree. The sprawling branches offer respite from the sun, a perfect setting for reflection on a life richly lived.

More than just the construction of houses, Henry's carpentry shaped his existence; he built homes, nurturing strong relationships with family and friends, and crafting lasting memories that continue to resonate. These memories, interwoven with the grain of the wood he worked so diligently, are the foundation of his contentment. He finds immense joy in sharing the wisdom gleaned from his years of experience with the neighborhood children.

Gathering around him, they listen attentively as he imparts life lessons, emphasizing the importance of honesty, hard work, and kindness—values that have served as his guiding principles throughout his journey. He speaks of the satisfaction of a job well done, not just in the physical structures he created, but also in the relationships he carefully constructed. He relates anecdotes from his past, illustrating how these principles have steered him through both challenges and triumphs.

His stories are not merely tales, but living examples of a life well-lived, a testament to the enduring power of integrity and compassion. The children, captivated by his stories and gentle demeanor, leave him each day with a deeper understanding of the world and a renewed appreciation for the simple yet profound truths he imparts. The oak tree, a silent witness to these afternoon gatherings, stands as a symbol of the enduring legacy Henry is leaving behind–a legacy built not only of wood and nails, but of kindness, honesty, and hard work.

Memorable Quote:

"The greatest gift of life is the wisdom that grows within us."–Unkn own.

Readers might reflect: *What wisdom have I gained through my journey, and how can I use it to inspire and shape others?*

Theme 2: Living Richly in the Present Moment

A life well lived isn't measured by what we achieve—it's measured by how deeply we experience each moment. The South, with its porch gatherings and slow summer evenings, teaches us to embrace the present with open hearts and grateful minds. Living richly isn't about rushing toward the next goal; it's about savoring the beauty of where we are.

Ruth, a grandmother with silver hair that catches the afternoon sun, sits on her porch, a weathered rocking chair creaking gently beneath her. In her lap rests a large bowl brimming with plump, green peas. She works slowly, her nimble fingers expertly shelling each pea, the rhythmic *pop* a gentle counterpoint to the children's laughter echoing from the nearby yard.

The children, a kaleidoscope of bright clothes and boundless energy, chase butterflies and shriek with delight as they play hopscotch on the worn flagstones. Their carefree joy mingles with the scent of honeysuckle and freshly cut grass, creating a tapestry of summer contentment. Ruth doesn't rush. She takes her time, savoring the warmth of the sun on her face, the feel of the cool peas in her hands, and the muted satisfaction of a task completed with mindful intention.

Each shelled pea is a small meditation, a reminder to slow down, to appreciate the simple beauty of the moment. The sun-drenched afternoon stretches languidly before her, punctuated by the occasional chirp of a cricket and the distant rumble of a lawnmower. Her quiet presence, a beacon of calm amidst the children's boisterous play, subtly encourages those around her to embrace the same peaceful rhythm, to find joy in the everyday, to live life with intention, one shelled pea at a time. The overflowing bowl, a testament to her gentle persistence, eventually becomes a symbol of the rich harvest of life's slower, more deliberate moments.

Memorable Quote:

"Be happy for this moment. This moment is your life."–Omar Khayyam.

Readers might reflect: *How can I live more fully in the present moment, appreciating the beauty and meaning it holds?*

Savoring Life's Connections

Living richly in the present also means savoring the relationships that shape our lives. This Southern philosophy emphasizes the importance of human connection, highlighting the simple yet profound joys found in shared experiences. Whether it's a leisurely meal enjoyed with loved ones, a quiet conversation that fosters understanding and intimacy, or a spontaneous moment of laughter that strengthens bonds, the South teaches us to value these connections as some of life's greatest blessings.

These interactions, far from being mere distractions, are integral to a fulfilling and meaningful life, enriching our days and leaving lasting positive effects. The emphasis is on quality time spent nurturing relationships, fostering a sense of belonging and community, and creating lasting memories. Therefore, we measure the richness of life not solely by material possessions, but by the depth and quality of our relationships.

Readers might ask: *Who in my life can I share a meaningful moment with today, and how can I cherish the connection we build?*

Memorable Quote:

"We do not remember days; we remember moments."–Cesare Pavese.

Theme 3: Building a Legacy of Meaning

A life well lived doesn't end with us—it continues through the legacy we leave behind. The South, with its emphasis on family, tradition, and connection, reminds us that our actions, words, and values shape not only our present but also the future of those who follow. Building a legacy isn't about fame or fortune—it's about living in ways that inspire, nurture, and connect.

Walter, the unassuming principal of a small Southern school, dedicated decades to quietly mentoring his students. He wasn't driven by a thirst for recognition; his motivation stemmed from a deep-seated belief in the transformative power of education and the importance of unwavering encouragement. He fostered a nurturing environment where students felt seen and valued, regardless of their background or aspirations.

His quiet influence shaped the lives of countless individuals who achieved remarkable success in diverse fields. Former students, now doctors, artists, farmers, and teachers themselves, frequently credited Walter as the pivotal figure who inspired them to pursue their dreams and reach their full potential.

Therefore, the community he served wove his legacy into its fabric, living in the hearts and lives he profoundly touched. His impact transcends mere statistics and academic achievements; it's a testament to the enduring power of mentorship and the muted dedication of a man who understood the true meaning of making a difference.

Memorable Quote:

"The great use of life is to spend it for something that will outlast it."–William James.

Living for Those Who Follow

In the journey of life, every action we take and every decision we make carries the potential to shape the legacy we leave for future generations. By living with purpose and intention, we create a gift that transcends time and enriches the lives of those who come after us.

The essence of our legacy lies not only in the material possessions we pass down, but in the intangible treasures of values, traditions, and memories that we leave behind. Drawing inspiration from the wisdom of the South, we learn it is often the insignificant acts that have the most profound impact. Planting a tree today may provide shade for generations to come, just as sharing a story can weave a thread of connection through the tapestry of family history. By extending a helping hand in times of need, we create ripples of kindness that resonate far beyond our own existence.

As we ponder how to live a life of lasting kindness, connection, and meaning, we should reflect on our daily choices. How can we cultivate compassion in our interactions with others? How can we nurture relationships that transcend boundaries of time and space? How can we infuse our actions with purpose and significance so that they reverberate through the lives of those who follow us?

By embracing the power of intentional living, we can shape a legacy that speaks to the best of who we are and what we stand for. Let us strive to be mindful of the impact we have on the world and to leave behind a legacy that is a beacon of light for generations yet to come.

Memorable Quote:

"What you leave behind is not what is engraved in stone monuments, but what is woven into the lives of others."–Pericles.

Final Reflection: The Legacy of a Life Well Lived

A life well lived is not about perfection, but about presence—living each day with intention, cherishing the moments that matter, and leaving behind a legacy of connection and meaning. The South teaches us that life's greatest riches are found not in material wealth, but in the relationships we nurture, the wisdom we gain, and the love we share.

As we conclude this chapter, we are reminded that a life well lived is one that touches hearts, inspires minds, and strengthens communities. It's a life rooted in authenticity and gratitude, where even the simplest acts carry a profound impact. May we each strive to live richly, embracing the present, honoring the past, and building a future filled with hope and purpose.

A Life Well Lived

Charles E. Cravey

A porch swing creaks, the evening's grace.
A life well lived is not a race.
It's measured not by steps we take.
But by the hearts, we gently wake.

In wisdom's fold, in moments near,
In every laugh, in every tear.
It's found in kindness, sweet and slow,
In planting seeds that time will grow.

Oh, South, you sing this muted tune,
Beneath the stars, beneath the moon.
A legacy of love you weave,
A treasure rich for hearts that grieve.

To live with truth, with hope, with care,
To find life's meaning everywhere.
This is the gift the South bestows,
A life well lived, in full repose.

Epilogue

The Bridge Beyond

"What we do for ourselves dies with us. What we do for others and the world remains and is immortal."—Albert Pine.

Life is a journey, a bridge built not for solitude but for connection, not for fleeting accomplishments but for lasting impact. As we cross this bridge, we carry with us the echoes of wisdom, courage, and love, knowing that the mark we leave behind is not in the monuments we build but in the hearts we touch.

The chapters of this journey have guided us through courage, purpose, resilience, grace, and reflection—truths deeply rooted in the wisdom of the South. Together, they have painted a portrait of what it means to live not just well, but fully. The South, with its traditions steeped in connection and its stories whispered beneath ancient oaks, teaches us to find meaning in the everyday, to honor the rhythms of life, and to embrace the values that shape us.

As we reach the bridge's crest, we look back: at the garden tended with care, the porch where laughter echoed, the quiet moments of reflection that revealed truths about ourselves. These are the treasures we take forward, woven into the fabric of who we are and who we're becoming. But the journey doesn't end here—it extends into the future, inviting us to carry these lessons onward, to plant new seeds, to build new connections, and to live with an ever-deepening sense of intention and grace.

A life well lived is not a destination; it is a continual unfolding, an ever-evolving story. And as we step into tomorrow, may we do so with open hearts, guided by the light within, and inspired by the timeless truths that have shaped this work.

Let this epilogue be a reminder, not of an ending, but of a beginning—an invitation to step boldly onto the bridge beyond, carrying with us all that we have learned and all that we have yet to discover.

The Bridge Beyond

Charles E. Cravey

A bridge of oak and whispered lore,
It spans the past and beckons more.
Each step is carved with hands that gave,
Their love, their light, their truths to save.

From soil to sky, from dusk to dawn,
We cross the bridge; we carry on.
The South's sweet voice, a guiding tune,
Through summer's sun and winter's moon.

It whispers soft, "Oh, live with care.
The bridge you build is always there.
For hearts you touch, for paths you mend,
The bridge of life will never end."

So, walk with courage, plant with grace,
Leave kindness in each fleeting space.

For as we cross, we come to see,
The bridge beyond is legacy.

About the author

The Reverend Doctor Charles Edward Cravey was born in Eastman, Georgia, to Carise Lee and Irene Cooper Cravey in 1951. In his lifetime, Dr. Cravey has lived in Milan, Helena, McRae, Cochran, Fitzgerald, Newington, Dublin, Bartow, Alamo, Warner Robins, Reidsville, Tifton, Millen, Macon, Sylvania, Lyons, Midville, and Statesboro, Georgia. He served United Methodist Churches for fifty-two years before retiring to Statesboro.

He is married to the love of his life, Charlotte Renee Dennis Cravey. They have two children: Angela Marie Cravey Monahan, who teaches kindergarten in Statesboro, and Jonathan Edward Cravey, who is a mechanical engineer in Sandy Springs (Atlanta), Georgia. The couple has two grandchildren, Meghan Marie Monahan and Benjamin Matthew Monahan, and they live in Statesboro.

Dr. Cravey has, to this date, written forty-six books, including children's books, seven novels, several novellas, devotional books, poetry books, and theological studies. He has been widely read and has won several awards for his writings, and his articles have appeared in various newspapers for years. He has won the prestigious PUBLISHERS CHOICE AWARD for this and several other books and continues to write daily.

Dr. Cravey has traveled extensively in mission work and ministry, having been in Costa Rica, Nicaragua, Panama, Ecuador, Venezuela,

Guyana, Honduras, Belize, Mexico, the islands of the Caribbean, Spain, France, and England, leading mission teams to build churches in those areas. He has served as the conference chair of missions and was past president for the Conference Volunteers in Missions committee. He traveled to the Holy Land on three separate occasions.

He has written several church anthems and Christian gospel songs, recorded seventeen gospel albums, and has written several official county songs throughout Georgia and South Carolina. He produced over forty albums for other Christian artists while owner of Upper Room Studios.

He has been the founder and owner of In His Steps Publishing Company and Headlight Press for over forty years. He was founder and president for the Society of American Poets and The Poet's Pen for many years before its demise upon the author's retirement.

His greatest quest is to leave the world a little better than he found it. Religion and Philosophy is his two greatest subjects.

You may find other Books by Dr. Cravey at Amazon.com or Https://drcharlescravey.com

www.ingramcontent.com/pod-product-compliance
Lightning Source LLC
Chambersburg PA
CBHW030930090426
42737CB00007B/377